BOB DYLAN THE LYRICS 1961–

LIKE A
ROLLING ST

像一块滚石

鲍勃·迪伦诗歌集 1961—2020
VOL.03

[美] 鲍勃·迪伦 著　李皖 译

中信出版集团｜北京

全部带回家
BRINGING IT ALL BACK HOME

地下乡愁蓝调	7
她是我的	15
玛吉的农场	19
爱减零/无限	23
亡命徒蓝调	27
再次上路	31
鲍勃·迪伦的第115个梦	35
铃鼓手先生	49
伊甸园之门	55
没事儿,妈(我不过是在流血)	61
一切结束了,蓝宝宝	71

—— 附加歌词 ——

加利福尼亚	75
别了安吉丽娜	79
爱不过就是个脏字	85

重访61号公路
HIGHWAY 61 REVISITED

像一块滚石	95
墓碑布鲁斯	101
要笑不容易,要哭只需坐火车	111

目录

来自别克 6	115
瘦子的歌谣	119
准女王简	127
重访 61 号公路	131
恰似大拇指汤姆蓝调	135
荒芜巷	141

------ 附加歌词 ------

准是第四街	153
能不能请你从窗子爬出去？	159
坐在带刺铁篱上	163

金发叠金发
BLONDE ON BLONDE

雨天女人 12 与 35 号	173
抵押我的时间	177
乔安娜的幻影	181
我们总有一个人要明白（迟早的事）	187
我要你	191
再次困在莫比尔和孟菲斯蓝调一起	197
豹皮药盒帽	207
就像个女人	211
多半是你走你的道（而我过我的桥）	215
像阿喀琉斯一样短命	219
绝对的甜蜜玛丽	223

第四次左右	227
分明五位信徒	231
低地的愁容夫人	235

---附加歌词---

我会把它当自己的事	241
我要做你情人	245
告诉我,妈妈	249
她现在是你的人了	255

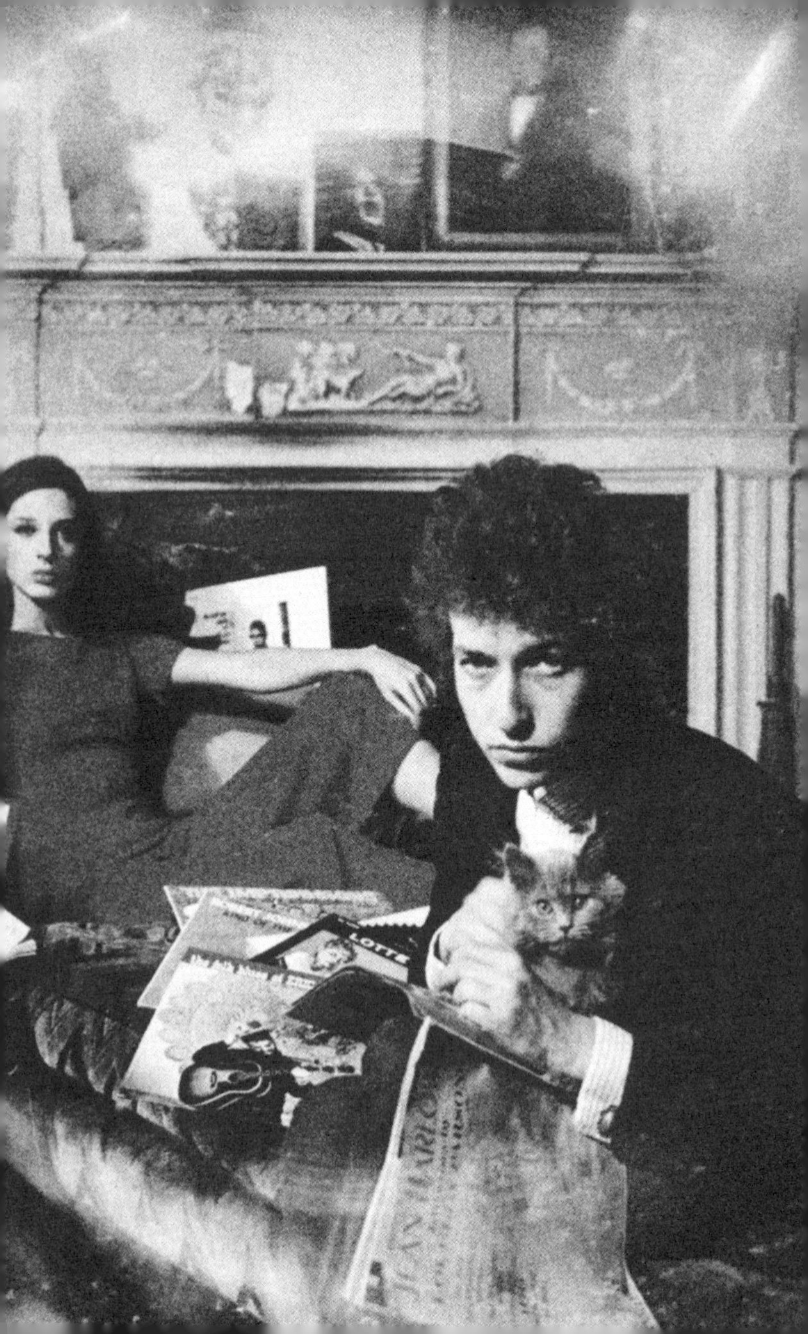
LOTTE

BRINGING IT ALL BACK HOME
全部带回家

地下乡愁蓝调

她是我的

玛吉的农场

爱减零 / 无限

亡命徒蓝调

再次上路

鲍勃·迪伦的第 115 个梦

铃鼓手先生

伊甸园之门

没事儿,妈(我不过是在流血)

一切结束了,蓝宝宝

附加歌词

加利福尼亚 爱不过就是个脏字
别了安吉丽娜

~~itxxxxii~~ I'd talk all nite to you but soon my words would turn into a
                              meaningless ring
for deep in my heart I know there's no help I can bring
everything passes. everything changes just do what you think you should do
~~for~~ someday baby who know maybe I'll come an be cryin t you.

just t add
tall + thein tline

《全部带回家》是迪伦的第5张录音室专辑，由哥伦比亚唱片公司于1965年3月22日发行。"全部带回家"这个标题，在英文原文中有一种决绝之意。这是第一次，迪伦用上了电声乐队。一般人能够意会，这是把乐器通上电。实质上，这还意味着迪伦将几乎完全由个人掌控的录音和演出交与团队完成。他的音乐方向也发生变化，民谣变成了摇滚乐；古老的、知识分子式的民歌变成了时髦的、青少年的流行乐。这是革命性的，犹如在民谣音乐界和知识分子群体中投下了一枚炸弹，引起了严重的观点分歧。

迪伦在思想上，或者说，在歌词上，此时也发生了显著变化。

1964年夏天，迪伦大部分时间都在纽约小镇伍德斯托克，他的经纪人艾伯特·格罗斯曼（Albert Grossman）的家中度过。专辑的大部分作品即写于这里。在此期间，迪伦的歌词变得越来越超现实；他的散文越来越个人化，近似于意识流写作。有时他半夜醒来跌跌撞撞地走向打字机，打下一些文字。他于1964年发表的信件，其含义随着时间的推移，变得越来越难以理解。

1964年8月28日，在纽约德尔莫尼科酒店，迪伦与

3

披头士乐队第一次会面。此后，英美流行音乐的两个巨头一直保持着良好的私人友谊，形成了彼此影响、良性互动和积极竞争的关系。

1965年1月13至15日，这张专辑共进行了4场录音，除了第一场，都是迪伦与电声乐队合作。据摄影师丹尼尔·克莱默（Daniel Kramer）回忆："音乐家们都很热情，他们彼此协商解决问题。迪伦从一人跳向另一人，解释自己想要什么，他时常在钢琴上做演示，向其他人展示自己需要什么，直到整首歌像一个巨大拼图，碎片被拼合起来，形象完整浮现……大多数歌曲容易把握，只需三四次录音……有时候，第一次录音听起来与最后一次完全不同，因为素材以不同速度被演奏，或选用了不同的和弦，或独奏被重新编排……迪伦的工作方法，以及他对自己想要的东西的笃定，让事情得以顺利进行。"[1]

专辑分为正反两面，由电声和原声两个部分组成。正面的歌曲由迪伦与电声摇滚乐队一起演奏，反面的歌曲则以迪伦自己的木吉他为主奏。迪伦进一步放弃了之前的抗议歌曲式的创作，转而采用更超现实、更复杂的歌词。演唱者的角色，从群体的代言人，进一步转向个人，转向迪伦自己。

超现实表达、纷繁意象和晦涩隐喻，不仅出现在反映时代主题的作品如《地下乡愁蓝调》《伊甸园之门》《铃鼓手先生》《一切结束了，蓝宝宝》中，也出现在个人抒情作

---

[1] "How Bob Dylan made 'Bringing It All Back Home' in three days". faroutmagazine.co.uk. March 22, 2022. Retrieved November 6, 2022.

品如《她是我的》《爱减零/无限》中。研究者注意到，这些作品不仅受到了法国诗人兰波的影响，也有英国诗人威廉·布莱克、美国作家和诗人爱伦·坡的复杂印记。虽然他一直拒绝"旗手""代言人"等标签，但是迪伦的作品直击时代的力度和深度、洞察力和判断力、立意和创造性，在歌词领域罕有其匹。确实，他的写作得到了来自民歌和《圣经》的启示，界限不凡。

《玛吉的农场》《再次上路》《鲍勃·迪伦的第115个梦》以及在主题上不那么重要的《亡命徒蓝调》，都是源自民歌的创作，为现代民歌和布鲁斯音乐赋予了更加超现实主义的表达和更加荒诞离奇的变形。迪伦以轻巧的方式去迎击或解构重大主题的能力，源自民歌的讽刺性和通俗幽默感，这也是罕见的。

专辑中最长的歌曲，《没事儿，妈（我不过是在流血）》，至今评论界仍缺乏对它的清晰认识。这首歌呈现出的对"巨变时代"的观察与感受之宽广、磅礴、雄浑、深刻，至今没有另一首歌词或诗歌作品可与之并驾齐驱。它反映的巨变是全球性的，其价值仍值得我们深入认识。

《全部带回家》被许多评论者认为是那个年代最有影响力的专辑，是有史以来最伟大的专辑之一，其后出版的流行音乐专辑几乎没有哪张不受它的影响，它对当代文化和思想的冲击也波及了文化和艺术的其他领域。

这张专辑产生了十几首弃用作品，其中《加利福尼亚》《别了安吉丽娜》《爱不过就是个脏字》作为附加歌词被收录进来。

SUBTERRANEAN HOMESICK BLUES

Johnny's in the basement

Mixing up the medicine

I'm on the pavement

Thinking about the government

The man in the trench coat

Badge out, laid off

Says he's got a bad cough

Wants to get it paid off

Look out kid

It's somethin' you did

God knows when

But you're doin' it again

You better duck down the alley way

Lookin' for a new friend

The man in the coon-skin cap

In the big pen

Wants eleven dollar bills

You only got ten

Maggie comes fleet foot

地下乡愁蓝调 [1]

约翰尼在地下室
混合着药物
我在人行道上
思考着政府
那个穿军大衣的人
徽章掉了,被解雇了
说他咳得厉害
想弄点药把病治好
当心小伙子
你捅了娄子
天知道何时干的
但你又干了一次
最好躲巷子里去
找一个新相好
戴浣熊皮帽的男人
在大钢笔里 [1]
想要十一美元
你只有十美元

玛吉疾步走来

---

[1] 在大钢笔里,指坐牢。

Face full of black soot
Talkin' that the heat put
Plants in the bed but
The phone's tapped anyway
Maggie says that many say
They must bust in early May
Orders from the D.A.
Look out kid
Don't matter what you did
Walk on your tiptoes
Don't try "No-Doz"
Better stay away from those
That carry around a fire hose
Keep a clean nose
Watch the plain clothes
You don't need a weatherman
To know which way the wind blows

Get sick, get well
Hang around a ink well
Ring bell, hard to tell
If anything is goin' to sell
Try hard, get barred
Get back, write braille

满脸都是黑煤灰
说条子在床上
安放了绿植
反正电话被窃听了
玛吉说传言纷起
五月初会有突击搜查
是地方检察官的指示
当心小伙子
不管你干了什么
都要踮起脚走路
别试咖啡因
最好离那帮
抬消防水龙带的远点儿[1]
保持鼻子洁净
当心便衣
你不需要气象员
就该知道风朝哪边吹

昏了,好了
晃来晃去绕着油墨井
按门铃,难说清
真有什么能卖出去
尽力了,被拒了
掉转头,写盲文

---

[1] 在美国黑人民权运动中,抗议者遭高压消防水枪喷射。

Get jailed, jump bail

Join the army, if you fail

Look out kid

You're gonna get hit

But users, cheaters

Six-time losers

Hang around the theaters

Girl by the whirlpool

Lookin' for a new fool

Don't follow leaders

Watch the parkin' meters

Ah get born, keep warm

Short pants, romance, learn to dance

Get dressed, get blessed

Try to be a success

Please her, please him, buy gifts

Don't steal, don't lift

Twenty years of schoolin'

And they put you on the day shift

Look out kid

They keep it all hid

Better jump down a manhole

Light yourself a candle

Don't wear sandals

Try to avoid the scandals

投入大牢,保释逃跑
若不成事,参军去也
当心小伙子
你会挨揍
但是毒虫、骗子
六度输家
都在戏院四周晃悠
小妞趁乱行事
准备钓新傻瓜
别跟随领导
注意泊车码表

啊出生,保暖
短裤,浪漫,学跳舞
穿戴好,受祝福
努力成为成功人士
讨好伊,讨好他,买礼物
不偷摸,不盗窃
上学二十年
然后排你值白班
当心小伙子
他们隐瞒了所有事
最好跳进检修孔
自己点起蜡烛
不要穿凉鞋
尽量避开丑闻

Don't wanna be a bum

You better chew gum

The pump don't work

'Cause the vandals took the handles

别想成为废物
最好嚼嚼口香糖
水泵坏了
因为破坏分子拿走了手柄

SHE BELONGS TO ME

She's got everything she needs
She's an artist, she don't look back
She's got everything she needs
She's an artist, she don't look back
She can take the dark out of the nighttime
And paint the daytime black

You will start out standing
Proud to steal her anything she sees
You will start out standing
Proud to steal her anything she sees
But you will wind up peeking through her keyhole
Down upon your knees

She never stumbles
She's got no place to fall
She never stumbles
She's got no place to fall
She's nobody's child
The Law can't touch her at all

她是我的 [1]

她想要的她都有了
她是个艺术家,从不回头看
她想要的她都有了
她是个艺术家,从不回头看
她能把白天涂黑
用从夜间提取的黑暗

开始你会站着
骄傲地偷取她看到的一切
开始你会站着
骄傲地偷取她看到的一切
但是最后你会从她的钥匙孔窥探
两条腿跪着

她从不摔跟头
从不会在哪儿跌倒
她从不摔跟头
从不会在哪儿跌倒
她是没人管的孩子
法律碰不到她分毫

---

[1] 本篇由杨盈盈校译。

She wears an Egyptian ring
That sparkles before she speaks
She wears an Egyptian ring
That sparkles before she speaks
She's a hypnotist collector
You are a walking antique

Bow down to her on Sunday
Salute her when her birthday comes
Bow down to her on Sunday
Salute her when her birthday comes
For Halloween give her a trumpet
And for Christmas, buy her a drum

她戴一枚埃及戒指
她开口讲话它就发光
她戴一枚埃及戒指
她开口讲话它就发光
她是催眠师收藏家
你是会走路的古董

星期天向她鞠躬
生日时向她致敬
星期天向她鞠躬
生日时向她致敬
万圣节送她小号
而圣诞节,给她买只鼓

MAGGIE'S FARM

I ain't gonna work on Maggie's farm no more
No, I ain't gonna work on Maggie's farm no more
Well, I wake in the morning
Fold my hands and pray for rain
I got a head full of ideas
That are drivin' me insane
It's a shame the way she makes me scrub the floor
I ain't gonna work on Maggie's farm no more

I ain't gonna work for Maggie's brother no more
No, I ain't gonna work for Maggie's brother no more
Well, he hands you a nickel
He hands you a dime
He asks you with a grin
If you're havin' a good time
Then he fines you every time you slam the door
I ain't gonna work for Maggie's brother no more

I ain't gonna work for Maggie's pa no more
No, I ain't gonna work for Maggie's pa no more
Well, he puts his cigar
Out in your face just for kicks

玛吉的农场

我不会再去玛吉的农场干活
是的,我不会再去玛吉的农场干活
哦,早上我醒来
双手合十祈求下雨
脑子里一大堆念头
都快把我逼疯了
她叫我那个样子擦地板真丢人
我不会再去玛吉的农场干活

我不会再给玛吉的兄弟干活
是的,我不会再给玛吉的兄弟干活
哦,他给你五分钱
他给你一毛钱
咧嘴笑着问
你开不开心
然后在你每次摔门时罚你的款
我不会再给玛吉的兄弟干活

我不会再给玛吉的爸干活
是的,我不会再给玛吉的爸干活
哦,他把他的雪茄
喷在你脸上取乐

His bedroom window
It is made out of bricks
The National Guard stands around his door
Ah, I ain't gonna work for Maggie's pa no more

I ain't gonna work for Maggie's ma no more
No, I ain't gonna work for Maggie's ma no more
Well, she talks to all the servants
About man and God and law
Everybody says
She's the brains behind pa
She's sixty-eight, but she says she's twenty-four
I ain't gonna work for Maggie's ma no more

I ain't gonna work on Maggie's farm no more
No, I ain't gonna work on Maggie's farm no more
Well, I try my best
To be just like I am
But everybody wants you
To be just like them
They sing while you slave and I just get bored
I ain't gonna work on Maggie's farm no more

他卧室的窗子
是砖块砌的
门口周围全是国民警卫队
啊,我不会再给玛吉的爸干活

我不会再给玛吉的妈干活
是的,我不会再给玛吉的妈干活
哦,她对所有的佣人
大谈人、上帝和法律
每个人都说
她是爸背后的主脑
她六十八了,却说自己二十四
我不会再给玛吉的妈干活

我不会再去玛吉的农场干活
是的,我不会再去玛吉的农场干活
哦,我尽力而为
做我自己
但每个人都想要你
变得像他们
他们唱歌,而你在苦作,我觉得真无聊
我不会再去玛吉的农场干活

LOVE MINUS ZERO/NO LIMIT

My love she speaks like silence
Without ideals or violence
She doesn't have to say she's faithful
Yet she's true, like ice, like fire
People carry roses
Make promises by the hours
My love she laughs like the flowers
Valentines can't buy her

In the dime stores and bus stations
People talk of situations
Read books, repeat quotations
Draw conclusions on the wall
Some speak of the future
My love she speaks softly
She knows there's no success like failure
And that failure's no success at all

The cloak and dagger dangles
Madams light the candles

爱减零 / 无限 [1]

我的爱人她说话宛如沉默
不含理想也无暴力
她用不着说她是忠贞的
然而她是这样真,如同冰,如同火
人们奉献玫瑰
按小时作出承诺
我的爱人她笑靥如花
情人节礼物无法收买她

在一元店和汽车站
人们聊着形势
读书,重复着语录
在墙上下结论
一些人谈到了未来
我的爱人她轻言细语
她知道没有成功比得上失败
而失败根本不算成功

斗篷和短剑悬荡
女士们燃起蜡烛

---

[1] 标题可读成"爱减零除以无限"。

In ceremonies of the horsemen
Even the pawn must hold a grudge
Statues made of matchsticks
Crumble into one another
My love winks, she does not bother
She knows too much to argue or to judge

The bridge at midnight trembles
The country doctor rambles
Bankers' nieces seek perfection
Expecting all the gifts that wise men bring
The wind howls like a hammer
The night blows cold and rainy
My love she's like some raven
At my window with a broken wing

骑师仪式上
即使小卒也必心有不甘
火柴棒制成的雕像
彼此相互瓦解
我的爱人眨眨眼,不予理睬
她知道得太多,不想争辩和评判

午夜的桥轻轻摇晃
乡村医生四处游荡
银行家的侄女们追求完美
期待着聪明人送来所有赠礼
风像锤子般号叫
夜冷冷含雨吹着
我的爱人她宛如一只渡鸦
停在我窗前,折了一只翅膀

OUTLAW BLUES

Ain't it hard to stumble
And land in some funny lagoon?
Ain't it hard to stumble
And land in some muddy lagoon?
Especially when it's nine below zero
And three o'clock in the afternoon

Ain't gonna hang no picture
Ain't gonna hang no picture frame
Ain't gonna hang no picture
Ain't gonna hang no picture frame
Well, I might look like Robert Ford
But I feel just like a Jesse James

Well, I wish I was on some
Australian mountain range
Oh, I wish I was on some
Australian mountain range

亡命徒蓝调

跌跌撞撞地踏进
某个可笑的潟湖岂不是挺难办?
跌跌撞撞地踏进
某个泥泞的潟湖岂不是挺难办?
尤其是在零下九度的
下午三点

我不会挂照片
我不会挂相框
我不会挂照片
我不会挂相框
嗯,可能我长得像罗伯特·福特
可是我觉得我像杰西·詹姆斯 [1]

嗯,我希望我是在
澳大利亚的某条山脉上
噢,我希望我是在
澳大利亚的某条山脉上

---

[1] 这首诗提到的两个人物,均为19世纪美国西部著名悍匪,詹姆斯尤为传奇。福特为詹姆斯的手下。为了获取巨额赏金,福特趁詹姆斯往墙上挂相框背对着他时,开枪将其射杀。

I got no reason to be there, but I
Imagine it would be some kind of change

I got my dark sunglasses
I got for good luck my black tooth
I got my dark sunglasses
I'm carryin' for good luck my black tooth
Don't ask me nothin' about nothin'
I just might tell you the truth

I got a woman in Jackson
I ain't gonna say her name
I got a woman in Jackson
I ain't gonna say her name
She's a brown-skin woman, but I
Love her just the same

我没理由去那儿，但是我
想象这或许会有某种变化

我带着我的黑太阳镜
我的黑牙给我好运
我带着我的黑太阳镜
我的黑牙会给我好运
一切的一切都不要问我
或许我就会告诉你真相

我在杰克逊[1]有个女人
我不会讲她的名字
我在杰克逊有个女人
我不会讲她的名字
她是个棕皮肤女人，可是我
一样爱她

---

[1] 杰克逊，美国城市。

ON THE ROAD AGAIN

Well, I woke up in the morning
There's frogs inside my socks
Your mama, she's a-hidin'
Inside the icebox
Your daddy walks in wearin'
A Napoleon Bonaparte mask
Then you ask why I don't live here
Honey, do you have to ask?

Well, I go to pet your monkey
I get a face full of claws
I ask who's in the fireplace
And you tell me Santa Claus
The milkman comes in
He's wearing a derby hat
Then you ask why I don't live here
Honey, how come you have to ask me that?

Well, I asked for something to eat
I'm hungry as a hog

再次上路

哦,早上我醒来
有青蛙在袜子里
你妈妈,躲在
冰柜中
你爸爸走进来
戴着拿破仑·波拿巴的面具
然后你问我为什么不住这儿了
亲爱的,你非要问吗?

哦,我去逗你的猴子
被弄得一脸血印
我问谁在壁炉里
你告诉我是圣诞老人
送奶工进来了
戴着一顶常礼帽[1]
然后你问我为什么不住这儿了
亲爱的,你为什么非要问这个?

哦,我要了些吃的
饿得像头猪

---

[1] 常礼帽,圆顶窄边的礼帽。

So I get brown rice, seaweed
And a dirty hot dog
I've got a hole
Where my stomach disappeared
Then you ask why I don't live here
Honey, I gotta think you're really weird

Your grandpa's cane
It turns into a sword
Your grandma prays to pictures
That are pasted on a board
Everything inside my pockets
Your uncle steals
Then you ask why I don't live here
Honey, I can't believe that you're for real

Well, there's fistfights in the kitchen
They're enough to make me cry
The mailman comes in
Even he's gotta take a side
Even the butler
He's got something to prove
Then you ask why I don't live here
Honey, how come you don't move?

所以我弄了糙米、海藻
还有一只脏热狗
我有个洞
我的胃在那儿消失了
然后你问我为什么不住这儿了
亲爱的，我觉得你真的好奇怪

你爷爷的拐杖
变成了一把剑
你奶奶对着贴在板子上的
画儿祈祷
我衣袋里的所有东西
你叔叔都要偷
然后你问我为什么不住这儿了
亲爱的，我不敢相信你是认真的

哦，厨房里有人打架
那场面让我叫喊
邮递员进来了
连他也要选边
甚至是管家
都搞得要证明什么
然后你问我为什么不住这儿了
亲爱的，你怎么还不走？

BOB DYLAN'S 115TH DREAM

I was riding on the Mayflower
When I thought I spied some land
I yelled for Captain Arab
I have yuh understand
Who came running to the deck
Said, "Boys, forget the whale
Look on over yonder
Cut the engines
Change the sail
Haul on the bowline"
We sang that melody
Like all tough sailors do
When they are far away at sea

"I think I'll call it America"
I said as we hit land
I took a deep breath
I fell down, I could not stand
Captain Arab he started

鲍勃·迪伦的第 115 个梦

当时我正乘着"五月花"号
我想我发现了一片大陆
我喊阿拉伯船长 [1]
我得让你明白
船长跑到甲板上
说:"孩儿们,别管鲸鱼了
瞧那边!
关掉发动机
变向
升帆"
我们唱起那支歌
像所有的糙哥儿水手
在远航时唱的那样

"我觉得我该叫它亚美利加"
登上陆地我说
我深吸了一口气
跌倒了,站不起来了
阿拉伯船长开始

---

[1] 阿拉伯船长,可能指美国作家梅尔维尔小说《白鲸》中的主角船长,叫亚哈船长(Captain Ahab)。

Writing up some deeds
He said, "Let's set up a fort
And start buying the place with beads"
Just then this cop comes down the street
Crazy as a loon
He throw us all in jail
For carryin' harpoons

Ah me I busted out
Don't even ask me how
I went to get some help
I walked by a Guernsey cow
Who directed me down
To the Bowery slums
Where people carried signs around
Saying, "Ban the bums"
I jumped right into line
Sayin', "I hope that I'm not late"
When I realized I hadn't eaten
For five days straight

I went into a restaurant

草拟契约
他说:"我们要建座城堡
还要用珠子置地"
这时候一个警察从街上跑过来
完全是发神经
把我们都投进监牢
就因为我们带了鱼叉

啊,我逃出来了
别问我怎么做成的
我去找帮手
路遇一头根西奶牛
它把我引到
包厘街[1]的贫民窟
到处都是人举着牌子
上写:"禁止流浪汉"[2]
我跳进队伍说
"但愿我没迟到"
这时我才意识到
我已经五天没吃东西了

我进了家餐馆

---

[1] 包厘街,纽约的一条街。
[2] "禁止流浪汉"(Ban the bums),谐音"禁止核武器"(ban the bombs)。

Lookin' for the cook
I told them I was the editor
Of a famous etiquette book
The waitress he was handsome
He wore a powder blue cape
I ordered some suzette, I said
"Could you please make that crepe"
Just then the whole kitchen exploded
From boilin' fat
Food was flying everywhere
And I left without my hat

Now, I didn't mean to be nosy
But I went into a bank
To get some bail for Arab
And all the boys back in the tank
They asked me for some collateral
And I pulled down my pants
They threw me in the alley
When up comes this girl from France
Who invited me to her house
I went, but she had a friend
Who knocked me out

找厨师
我告诉他们我是编辑
编过一本著名礼仪书
女服务生他很帅 [1]
穿着件浅蓝色斗篷
我点了叙泽特 [2],说
"你们能做那种可丽饼吧"
就在这时整个厨房
被沸油引爆
食物到处飞
我没拿帽子就走了

瞧,我无意多管闲事
但我去了一家银行
想为阿拉伯船长和号子里的
所有兄弟搞点保释金
他们向我要抵押品
我脱下裤子
他们就把我扔进了巷子
这时来了位法国妹子
邀我去她家里
我去了,但她有个朋友
把我打晕了

---

[1] 原文如此,性别含混。
[2] 叙泽特,一种饼,以黄油、橙汁并浇以烈酒烧灼制成。

And robbed my boots
And I was on the street again

Well, I rapped upon a house
With the U.S. flag upon display
I said, "Could you help me out
I got some friends down the way"
The man says, "Get out of here
I'll tear you limb from limb"
I said, "You know they refused Jesus, too"
He said, "You're not Him
Get out of here before I break your bones
I ain't your pop"
I decided to have him arrested
And I went looking for a cop

I ran right outside
And I hopped inside a cab
I went out the other door
This Englishman said, "Fab"
As he saw me leap a hot dog stand
And a chariot that stood
Parked across from a building

还抢走了我的靴子
然后我又回到街上

好吧,我敲着一家房门
上面有美国国旗
我说:"你能帮帮我吗?
我有些朋友遇上了麻烦"
那人说:"滚开
看我把你撕成碎片"
我说:"你知道他们也拒绝过耶稣"
他说:"你不是他
在我打断你骨头之前快滚
我又不是你老子"
我决定让人逮捕他
然后就去找警察

我径直跑到外面
跳上一辆出租车
从另一扇门下车
有个英国人说:"帅极了"[1]
他看着我跳过热狗摊
又跳过停在一栋楼
对面的马车

---

[1] 这里说玩笑话,指涉披头士乐队为甩掉歌迷,以车队为障碍,从车的一侧开门进入,从另一侧开门逃出去。

Advertising brotherhood
I ran right through the front door
Like a hobo sailor does
But it was just a funeral parlor
And the man asked me who I was

I repeated that my friends
Were all in jail, with a sigh
He gave me his card
He said, "Call me if they die"
I shook his hand and said goodbye
Ran out to the street
When a bowling ball came down the road
And knocked me off my feet
A pay phone was ringing
It just about blew my mind
When I picked it up and said hello
This foot came through the line

Well, by this time I was fed up
At tryin' to make a stab
At bringin' back any help
For my friends and Captain Arab
I decided to flip a coin
Like either heads or tails
Would let me know if I should go

那栋楼宣扬着兄弟情谊
我直接从前门跑进去
就像流浪水手那样
但那只是座殡仪馆
那人问我是谁

我又说了一遍,我的朋友们
都在监狱里,他叹了口气
给了我他的名片
说:"若他们死了打我电话"
我握了握他的手说再见
跑到了街上
一个保龄球顺路滚来
把我撞倒了
公用电话铃声大作
让我吃了一惊
我拿起话筒回说喂
这只脚这时穿过了那道线

好了,这时候我受够了
就为了试一试
给朋友们和阿拉伯船长
争得一点儿帮助
我决定抛硬币
不管正面还是反面
都会让我知道我是该

43

Back to ship or back to jail
So I hocked my sailor suit
And I got a coin to flip
It came up tails
It rhymed with sails
So I made it back to the ship

Well, I got back and took
The parkin' ticket off the mast
I was ripping it to shreds
When this coastguard boat went past
They asked me my name
And I said, "Captain Kidd"
They believed me but
They wanted to know
What exactly that I did
I said for the Pope of Eruke
I was employed
They let me go right away
They were very paranoid

回船上还是回监狱
于是我典当了我的水手服
换来一枚硬币抛了起来
结果是反面
反和帆同韵
所以我决定回到船上 [1]

好啦，我回来啦
从桅杆上取下违停罚单
正要把它撕碎
海岸警卫队开了过来
他们问我叫什么
我说："基德船长" [2]
他们信了我但是
他们想知道
我具体干什么
我说我受雇于
伊鲁克的教皇 [3]
他们立马就让我走了
他们都是妄想狂

---

[1] 硬币的反面（tail）和船帆（sail）同韵，但其实也与监狱（jail）同韵。
[2] 历史上有位著名的苏格兰水手，威廉·基德（1645—1701），因海盗罪被处决。
[3] 迪伦杜撰的人物。

Well, the last I heard of Arab
He was stuck on a whale
That was married to the deputy
Sheriff of the jail
But the funniest thing was
When I was leavin' the bay
I saw three ships a-sailin'
They were all heading my way
I asked the captain what his name was
And how come he didn't drive a truck
He said his name was Columbus
I just said, "Good luck"

哦，我最后听说阿拉伯船长

迷上了一头鲸鱼[1]

那鲸鱼嫁给了

监狱的副警长

但最好笑的事情是

当我离开海湾时

看见了三艘船[2]

全沿着我的原路鼓帆驶来

我问船长尊姓大名

他怎么不开卡车[3]

他说他名叫哥伦布

我就说："祝你好运"

---

[1] 鲸鱼，俚语有"肥婆"之意。
[2] 哥伦布 1492 年"发现美洲"的船队，由 3 艘帆船组成。
[3] 这里也是逗乐，隐晦地指涉"猫王"，发迹之前为卡车司机。

MR. TAMBOURINE MAN

Hey! Mr. Tambourine Man, play a song for me
I'm not sleepy and there is no place I'm going to
Hey! Mr. Tambourine Man, play a song for me
In the jingle jangle morning I'll come followin' you

Though I know that evenin's empire has returned into sand
Vanished from my hand
Left me blindly here to stand but still not sleeping
My weariness amazes me, I'm branded on my feet
I have no one to meet
And the ancient empty street's too dead for dreaming

Hey! Mr. Tambourine Man, play a song for me
I'm not sleepy and there is no place I'm going to
Hey! Mr. Tambourine Man, play a song for me
In the jingle jangle morning I'll come followin' you

Take me on a trip upon your magic swirlin' ship
My senses have been stripped, my hands can't feel to grip
My toes too numb to step
Wait only for my boot heels to be wanderin'
I'm ready to go anywhere, I'm ready for to fade

铃鼓手先生

嘿!铃鼓手先生,为我弹首歌吧
我不想入睡可是也没地方去
嘿!铃鼓手先生,为我弹首歌吧
在叮叮当当的早晨,我将随你而去

虽然我知道黄昏的帝国已潜回沙土
从我手中消逝
撂下我茫然站在这里,却仍无睡意
疲倦令我吃惊,我的脚盖了印
再没什么人要见了
这古老的空空的街,对做梦而言,太死寂

嘿!铃鼓手先生,为我弹首歌吧
我不想入睡可是也没地方去
嘿!铃鼓手先生,为我弹首歌吧
在叮叮当当的早晨,我将随你而去

带我登上你的魔法涡轮,航行
我的感官被剥夺,手也感觉不到紧握
我的脚趾麻了,不能动
只等着随靴子漫游
我已准备好漂流四方,准备好隐入

Into my own parade, cast your dancing spell my way
I promise to go under it

Hey! Mr. Tambourine Man, play a song for me
I'm not sleepy and there is no place I'm going to
Hey! Mr. Tambourine Man, play a song for me
In the jingle jangle morning I'll come followin' you

Though you might hear laughin', spinnin', swingin' madly
   across the sun
It's not aimed at anyone, it's just escapin' on the run
And but for the sky there are no fences facin'
And if you hear vague traces of skippin' reels of rhyme
To your tambourine in time, it's just a ragged clown behind
I wouldn't pay it any mind
It's just a shadow you're seein' that he's chasing

Hey! Mr. Tambourine Man, play a song for me
I'm not sleepy and there is no place I'm going to
Hey! Mr. Tambourine Man, play a song for me
In the jingle jangle morning I'll come followin' you

Then take me disappearin' through the smoke rings of my mind
Down the foggy ruins of time, far past the frozen leaves
The haunted, frightened trees, out to the windy beach
Far from the twisted reach of crazy sorrow

一个人的游行,向我施展你的舞蹈咒语吧
我发誓将服从它

嘿!铃鼓手先生,为我弹首歌吧
我不想入睡可是也没地方去
嘿!铃鼓手先生,为我弹首歌吧
在叮叮当当的早晨,我将随你而去

虽然你可能听见笑声,疯狂地旋转、摇摆
 越过太阳
这并不针对任何人,只是一路逃跑、流亡
而除了天面前再无屏障
如果你听见那韵律跳跃着旋转的模糊印迹
在应和着你的铃鼓,那不过是衣衫褴褛的小丑跟在后面
我一点儿都不会搭理
他在追逐的只是你眼中的一个影子

嘿!铃鼓手先生,为我弹首歌吧
我不想入睡可是也没地方去
嘿!铃鼓手先生,为我弹首歌吧
在叮叮当当的早晨,我将随你而去

然后就带我消失吧,消失在我思想的烟圈中
沉入雾腾腾的时间废墟,远涉过冰封的落叶
鬼影幢幢的、受惊的树林,走向风的海滨
逃离狂悲缠绕之手

Yes, to dance beneath the diamond sky with one hand waving
   free
Silhouetted by the sea, circled by the circus sands
With all memory and fate driven deep beneath the waves
Let me forget about today until tomorrow

Hey! Mr. Tambourine Man, play a song for me
I'm not sleepy and there is no place I'm going to
Hey! Mr. Tambourine Man, play a song for me
In the jingle jangle morning I'll come followin' you

是的,在钻石天空下起舞,一只手自由
　舞动
圆形沙滩环绕,大海映出剪影
所有的记忆和命运被赶进深深的海浪
让我忘掉今天,直到明日来临

嘿!铃鼓手先生,为我弹首歌吧
我不想入睡可是也没地方去
嘿!铃鼓手先生,为我弹首歌吧
在叮叮当当的早晨,我将随你而去

GATES OF EDEN

Of war and peace the truth just twists
Its curfew gull just glides
Upon four-legged forest clouds
The cowboy angel rides
With his candle lit into the sun
Though its glow is waxed in black
All except when 'neath the trees of Eden

The lamppost stands with folded arms
Its iron claws attached
To curbs 'neath holes where babies wail
Though it shadows metal badge
All and all can only fall
With a crashing but meaningless blow
No sound ever comes from the Gates of Eden

The savage soldier sticks his head in sand
And then complains
Unto the shoeless hunter who's gone deaf
But still remains
Upon the beach where hound dogs bay
At ships with tattooed sails

伊甸园之门

关于战争与和平的真相都是扭曲的
它的宵禁的海鸥刚刚掠过
四条腿的森林云
牛仔天使骑坐在上面
手上的蜡烛被点亮成了太阳
尽管它的光辉被蜡染成了黑色
除了当他在伊甸园的树下时

灯柱抱臂而立
它的铁爪紧抓着
婴儿号哭的危房下的路阶
虽然它遮蔽了金属徽章
到头来却只会倒掉
带着一声轰然却无意义的巨响
伊甸园之门从不发出声响

蛮族战士把头插在沙子里
然后向那个
耳聋的赤脚猎人抱怨
猎人仍留守在海滩
猎犬冲着轮船吠叫
轮船挂着刺青的帆

Heading for the Gates of Eden

With a time-rusted compass blade
Aladdin and his lamp
Sits with Utopian hermit monks
Sidesaddle on the Golden Calf
And on their promises of paradise
You will not hear a laugh
All except inside the Gates of Eden

Relationships of ownership
They whisper in the wings
To those condemned to act accordingly
And wait for succeeding kings
And I try to harmonize with songs
The lonesome sparrow sings
There are no kings inside the Gates of Eden

The motorcycle black madonna
Two-wheeled gypsy queen
And her silver-studded phantom cause
The gray flannel dwarf to scream
As he weeps to wicked birds of prey
Who pick up on his bread crumb sins
And there are no sins inside the Gates of Eden

驶向那伊甸园之门

带着已被时间锈蚀的指南针片
阿拉丁和他的神灯
与乌托邦的隐居僧们一起
一起侧坐在金牛犊背上
但在他们对天堂的许诺里
你不会听到笑声
除非在伊甸园的门内

人类的所有权关系
俱在两翼中低语
让那些负罪的人照此行事
一边等待着继任的列王
而我试图以和声
配合寂寞麻雀所唱
伊甸园的门内没有诸王

摩托黑圣母
双轮吉卜赛女皇
以及她镶了银的幻影
都让灰色法兰绒侏儒惊叫
当他对着邪恶猛禽垂泪
猛禽们领悟了他的面包屑之罪
而伊甸园的门内没有罪

The kingdoms of Experience
In the precious wind they rot
While paupers change possessions
Each one wishing for what the other has got
And the princess and the prince
Discuss what's real and what is not
It doesn't matter inside the Gates of Eden

The foreign sun, it squints upon
A bed that is never mine
As friends and other strangers
From their fates try to resign
Leaving men wholly, totally free
To do anything they wish to do but die
And there are no trials inside the Gates of Eden

At dawn my lover comes to me
And tells me of her dreams
With no attempts to shovel the glimpse
Into the ditch of what each one means
At times I think there are no words
But these to tell what's true
And there are no truths outside the Gates of Eden

经验之王国
在一本正经的风中朽腐
穷光蛋们交换着财物
每人都想要对方拥有的
而公主和王子
争论着什么是真的什么不是
在伊甸园的门内这都无所谓

异国的太阳,斜视着一张
永远不属于我的床
当朋友们和其他陌生人
试图放弃其命运
让人完全、彻底地自由
去做除死之外任何想做的事
而伊甸园的门内没有审判

黎明时分我的爱人来到身边
对我讲述她的梦
她没有打算将闪念
铲进人人意谓的沟渠
有时我觉得除了这些
没有任何话能说出真实
而伊甸园的门外没有真实

IT'S ALRIGHT, MA
(I'M ONLY BLEEDING)

Darkness at the break of noon

Shadows even the silver spoon

The handmade blade, the child's balloon

Eclipses both the sun and moon

To understand you know too soon

There is no sense in trying

Pointed threats, they bluff with scorn

Suicide remarks are torn

From the fool's gold mouthpiece the hollow horn

Plays wasted words, proves to warn

That he not busy being born is busy dying

Temptation's page flies out the door

You follow, find yourself at war

Watch waterfalls of pity roar

You feel to moan but unlike before

You discover that you'd just be one more

Person crying

没事儿,妈
(我不过是在流血)[1]

正午初临时的黑暗
甚至遮蔽了银匙
手工刀片,孩童的气球
太阳和月亮同时被蚀去
要有所理解,你知道还太早
所有尝试都没有意义

尖锐的威胁,以轻蔑虚张声势
从白痴的金话筒
自杀言论变成了破音,这空洞的大喇叭
播放着废话,原来是通知
人若不奋力重生,便等于在奋力求死

诱惑之书飞出大门
你跟随着,发现自己置身一场战争
眼见着怜悯的瀑布轰然而落
你想呻吟,但是不像从前
你发现你不过是又一个
哭泣的人

---

[1] 本篇由郝佳校译。

So don't fear if you hear
A foreign sound to your ear
It's alright, Ma, I'm only sighing

As some warn victory, some downfall
Private reasons great or small
Can be seen in the eyes of those that call
To make all that should be killed to crawl
While others say don't hate nothing at all
Except hatred

Disillusioned words like bullets bark
As human gods aim for their mark
Make everything from toy guns that spark
To flesh-colored Christs that glow in the dark
It's easy to see without looking too far
That not much is really sacred

While preachers preach of evil fates
Teachers teach that knowledge waits
Can lead to hundred-dollar plates
Goodness hides behind its gates
But even the president of the United States
Sometimes must have to stand naked

所以别害怕,如果你听见
一个不熟悉的声音进入你耳鼓
没事儿,妈,我只是在叹息

有人宣告胜利,有人倒台
那些叫嚷着
"该死的人就应该爬"的家伙
眼中自有大大小小的道理
而其他的人则说,不要仇恨任何事物
除了仇恨本身

幻想破灭的言语像子弹呼啸
当人神指向他们的目标
创造出了一切,从闪烁的玩具枪
到荧光的肉色基督像
无须看得太远,这显而易见
没有多少东西是真正神圣的

传教士们宣讲着恶人的命运
教师们也说得头头是道
知识就是财富
美德就藏身在它的门后
但就是美利坚合众国总统
有时也不得不裸体站着

An' though the rules of the road have been lodged
It's only people's games that you got to dodge
And it's alright, Ma, I can make it

Advertising signs they con
You into thinking you're the one
That can do what's never been done
That can win what's never been won
Meantime life outside goes on
All around you

You lose yourself, you reappear
You suddenly find you got nothing to fear
Alone you stand with nobody near
When a trembling distant voice, unclear
Startles your sleeping ears to hear
That somebody thinks they really found you

A question in your nerves is lit
Yet you know there is no answer fit
To satisfy, insure you not to quit
To keep it in your mind and not forget
That it is not he or she or them or it
That you belong to

Although the masters make the rules

虽然路上有路上的规矩
但你还是要避开人与人的游戏
放心吧妈，我能行

广告牌把你忽悠得飘飘然
以为你就是那个
能做别人从没做过的事
赢别人从没赢过的人
但你周围的生活
一切如常继续

你失去了自己，你重新出现
突然发现自己已无所畏惧
你独自站着，身边没有一个人
一个遥远的战栗的声音
这时惊醒你昏睡的耳朵，它模糊地说
有人觉得他们真的找到了你

神经里的一个问题遂被点亮
虽然你知道这问题没有你满意的
合适答案，但千万不要放弃
要把它存在你心底不忘记
你不属于
他、她、他们或它

虽然主人们为聪明人和傻瓜

For the wise men and the fools
I got nothing, Ma, to live up to

For them that must obey authority
That they do not respect in any degree
Who despise their jobs, their destinies
Speak jealously of them that are free
Cultivate their flowers to be
Nothing more than something they invest in

While some on principles baptized
To strict party platform ties
Social clubs in drag disguise
Outsiders they can freely criticize
Tell nothing except who to idolize
And then say God bless him

While one who sings with his tongue on fire
Gargles in the rat race choir
Bent out of shape from society's pliers
Cares not to come up any higher
But rather get you down in the hole
That he's in

But I mean no harm nor put fault
On anyone that lives in a vault

都制定了规则
妈,我没什么,需要遵守

有些人不得不服从权威
虽然对权威一点儿瞧不起
他们看不上自己的工作和归宿
只会嫉妒地议论那些自由的人
培育鲜花对他们而言只是
投资,除此没有其他意义

有些人大谈受洗的原则
为纲领必须遵守
可加入的却是变相的社交俱乐部
让局外人自由地批评吧
他们只用挑一个偶像崇拜
然后说,愿上帝保佑他

有人巧舌如火地唱圣歌
却在追名逐利的唱诗班中漱口
在社会的老虎钳中改变形状
他们想上也上不来
所以只想拖住你,把你拖进
他所住的坑中

但我并不想伤害谁,也不想找碴儿
有些人就是生活在地穴下

But it's alright, Ma, if I can't please him

Old lady judges watch people in pairs
Limited in sex, they dare
To push fake morals, insult and stare
While money doesn't talk, it swears
Obscenity, who really cares
Propaganda, all is phony

While them that defend what they cannot see
With a killer's pride, security
It blows the minds most bitterly
For them that think death's honesty
Won't fall upon them naturally
Life sometimes must get lonely

My eyes collide head-on with stuffed
Graveyards, false gods, I scuff
At pettiness which plays so rough
Walk upside-down inside handcuffs
Kick my legs to crash it off
Say okay, I have had enough
What else can you show me?

And if my thought-dreams could be seen
They'd probably put my head in a guillotine
But it's alright, Ma, it's life, and life only

但是没事儿,妈,如果我不能取悦他

人老珠黄的女法官,监视着成双成对的伴侣
自己缺乏性生活
便对别人满嘴仁义道德,侮辱仇视
金钱不会说话,金钱却会骂人
它说下流,一切都是骗人的
甭去理会宣传

有些人用凶手的荣誉
保护着他们看不见的东西,但是安全感
其实痛苦得不可思议
那些认为坦然面对死亡
不会自然落到头上的人
生活有时必须变得孤独

我睁眼望去,到处是
拥挤的墓园,虚假的神,我拖着脚
踩着坑坑洼洼的鸡毛蒜皮
戴着镣铐头冲下脚朝天地走着
我踢着腿,想把镣铐挣脱
说好了好了,我已经够了
还有什么新玩意儿,没给我看?

如果我的思想之梦被人看见
也许它们会送我上断头台
但是没事儿,妈,这是生命,不过是生命

IT'S ALL OVER NOW, BABY BLUE

You must leave now, take what you need, you think will last
But whatever you wish to keep, you better grab it fast
Yonder stands your orphan with his gun
Crying like a fire in the sun
Look out the saints are comin' through
And it's all over now, Baby Blue

The highway is for gamblers, better use your sense
Take what you have gathered from coincidence
The empty-handed painter from your streets
Is drawing crazy patterns on your sheets
This sky, too, is folding under you
And it's all over now, Baby Blue

All your seasick sailors, they are rowing home
All your reindeer armies, are all going home
The lover who just walked out your door
Has taken all his blankets from the floor
The carpet, too, is moving under you
And it's all over now, Baby Blue

一切结束了,蓝宝宝 [1]

你得走了,带着你需要的,你以为会长久的
但不管想留什么,最好快一点儿抓到手
那边儿站着你的孤儿,手里握着枪
哭得就像太阳里的火
留神啊,圣徒们正走过来
现在一切结束了,蓝宝宝

公路是属于赌徒的,你最好凭直觉
拿走你碰巧采到的
你住的街区,两手空空的画家
正在你的床单上疯狂涂鸦
天空也塌下来,向你压下来
现在一切结束了,蓝宝宝

所有你的晕船的水手,都在划船回家
所有你的驯鹿大军,都在往家里跑
刚走出门的你的情人
从地板上收去了他的铺盖
地毯也动起来,在你身下移动
现在一切结束了,蓝宝宝

---

[1] 本篇由郝佳校译。

Leave your stepping stones behind, something calls for you
Forget the dead you've left, they will not follow you
The vagabond who's rapping at your door
Is standing in the clothes that you once wore
Strike another match, go start anew
And it's all over now, Baby Blue

把一块块垫脚石抛在身后,什么声音在向你呼唤
忘掉已经告别的亡人,他们不会再跟随你
正敲你房门的流浪汉
站在那里,身上穿着你以前的衣服
划燃另一根火柴,重新开始吧
现在一切结束了,蓝宝宝

CALIFORNIA
(EARLY VERSION OF "OUTLAW BLUES")

I'm goin' down south
'Neath the borderline
I'm goin' down south
'Neath the borderline
Some fat momma
Kissed my mouth one time

Well, I needed it this morning
Without a shadow of doubt
My suitcase is packed
My clothes are hangin' out

San Francisco's fine
You sure get lots of sun
San Francisco is fine
You sure get lots of sun
But I'm used to four seasons
California's got but one

Well, I got my dark sunglasses
I got for good luck my black tooth

加利福尼亚
(《亡命徒蓝调》早期版本)

我要去南方
到边境线下边去
我要去南方
到边境线下边去
有位胖妈妈
亲过我的嘴

嗯,今早我就走
不带一丝犹豫
行李箱收好了
衣服已经挂出去

旧金山天气好啊
一准晒够太阳
旧金山天气好啊
一准晒够太阳
只是我习惯了四季
加州只有一季

嗯,我带了黑色太阳镜
我有颗黑牙给我好运

I got my dark sunglasses
And for good luck I got my black tooth
Don't ask me nothin' about nothin'
I just might tell you the truth

我带了黑色太阳镜
我有颗黑牙为了求好运
一切的一切都不要问我
我可能就会告诉你真相

FAREWELL ANGELINA

Farewell Angelina
The bells of the crown
Are being stolen by bandits
I must follow the sound
The triangle tingles
And the trumpets play slow
Farewell Angelina
The sky is on fire
And I must go

There's no need for anger
There's no need for blame
There's nothing to prove
Ev'rything's still the same
Just a table standing empty
By the edge of the sea
Farewell Angelina
The sky is trembling
And I must leave

别了安吉丽娜 [1]

别了安吉丽娜
王冠上的铃铛
被盗贼窃走了
我必须追随那声音
三角铁叮叮咚咚
小号缓缓吹着
别了安吉丽娜
天空着火了
我得走了

生气没必要
责备没必要
没什么要证明的
一切还是老样子
只有一张桌子
空空地立在大海边缘
别了安吉丽娜
天空在颤抖
我得走了

---

[1] 本篇由杨盈盈校译。

The jacks and the queens
Have forsaked the courtyard
Fifty-two gypsies
Now file past the guards
In the space where the deuce
And the ace once ran wild
Farewell Angelina
The sky is folding
I'll see you in a while

See the cross-eyed pirates sitting
Perched in the sun
Shooting tin cans
With a sawed-off shotgun
And the neighbors they clap
And they cheer with each blast
Farewell Angelina
The sky's changing color
And I must leave fast

King Kong, little elves
On the rooftops they dance

侍从和皇后们

已经抛弃这个院落

五十二个吉卜赛人

现在鱼贯越过了警卫

在两点和 A 点

曾经横行的那一段

别了安吉丽娜

天空在折起

我们一会儿见 [1]

看,坐着的对眼儿海盗们

栖息在阳光里

用锯短了枪管的火枪

射罐头盒

而邻居们鼓着掌

为每次击中欢呼

别了安吉丽娜

天空在变色

我必须赶快走

金刚、小精灵们

在屋顶上跳着

---

[1] 这段借用了扑克牌在叙事,侍从(J)、皇后(Q)、两点(2)和 A 点(A),都是扑克牌的牌面。两点和 A 点,又指网球比赛中的平局(双方各得 40 分)和爱司球(发球得分)。

Valentino-type tangos
While the makeup man's hands
Shut the eyes of the dead
Not to embarrass anyone
Farewell Angelina
The sky is embarrassed
And I must be gone

The machine guns are roaring
The puppets heave rocks
The fiends nail time bombs
To the hands of the clocks
Call me any name you like
I will never deny it
Farewell Angelina
The sky is erupting
I must go where it's quiet

瓦伦蒂诺式探戈
当化妆师的手
为死者阖上眼帘
以不使任何人不安
别了安吉丽娜
天空感到不安
我得走了

机枪在咆哮
木偶们投掷石块
恶魔将定时炸弹
连在时钟指针上
随你怎么称呼我
我都不会不认
别了安吉丽娜
天空在爆发
我必须去安静所在

LOVE IS JUST A FOUR LETTER WORD

Seems like only yesterday
I left my mind behind
Down in the Gypsy Café
With a friend of a friend of mine
She sat with a baby heavy on her knee
Yet spoke of life most free from slavery
With eyes that showed no trace of misery
A phrase in connection first with she I heard
That love is just a four letter word

Outside a rambling storefront window
Cats meowed to the break of day
Me, I kept my mouth shut, too
To you I had no words to say
My experience was limited and underfed
You were talking while I hid
To the one who was the father of your kid
You probably didn't think I did, but I heard
You say that love is just a four letter word

爱不过就是个脏字 [1]

依稀就像在昨日
我将心中诸念抛下
走进吉卜赛人咖啡馆
去见一个朋友的朋友
她坐在那儿,婴儿重重压在膝上
谈论起生活,却全无被束缚的神色
眼中不见一丝愁苦
我听到的这句话最早跟她有关
爱不过就是个脏字

在凌乱的店面窗户外面
几只猫叫到了天亮
而我,一直缄口不语
对你无话可讲
我的阅历有限,可说是贫乏
你对那个人,你孩子的父亲
说话时,我一直躲避着
可能你以为我没有,可我确实听到了
你说爱不过就是个脏字

---

[1] 本篇由杨盈盈校译。

I said goodbye unnoticed
Pushed towards things in my own games
Drifting in and out of lifetimes
Unmentionable by name
Searching for my double, looking for
Complete evaporation to the core
Though I tried and failed at finding any door
I must have thought that there was nothing more
Absurd than that love is just a four letter word

Though I never knew just what you meant
When you were speaking to your man
I can only think in terms of me
And now I understand
After waking enough times to think I see
The Holy Kiss that's supposed to last eternity
Blow up in smoke, its destiny
Falls on strangers, travels free
Yes, I know now, traps are only set by me
And I do not really need to be
Assured that love is just a four letter word

我不声不响地作别
将一切推向我自己的游戏
漂进漂出于
无以名状的诸种人生
搜索着自己的同款,寻找着
完全彻底的人间蒸发之途
试着得其门径,却终告失败
我当时一定以为,再没有什么
会比这更荒谬:爱不过就是个脏字

尽管我从不明白你是何意
当你和你的男人说话
而我只会从我的角度考虑
但现在我明白了
在无数次醒来思考之后,我看到
那本该意味着永恒的圣吻
化成了烟,它的命运
落到陌生人身上,四处飘散
是的,现在我懂了,都是我在自设牢笼
我真的没必要相信
爱不过就是个脏字

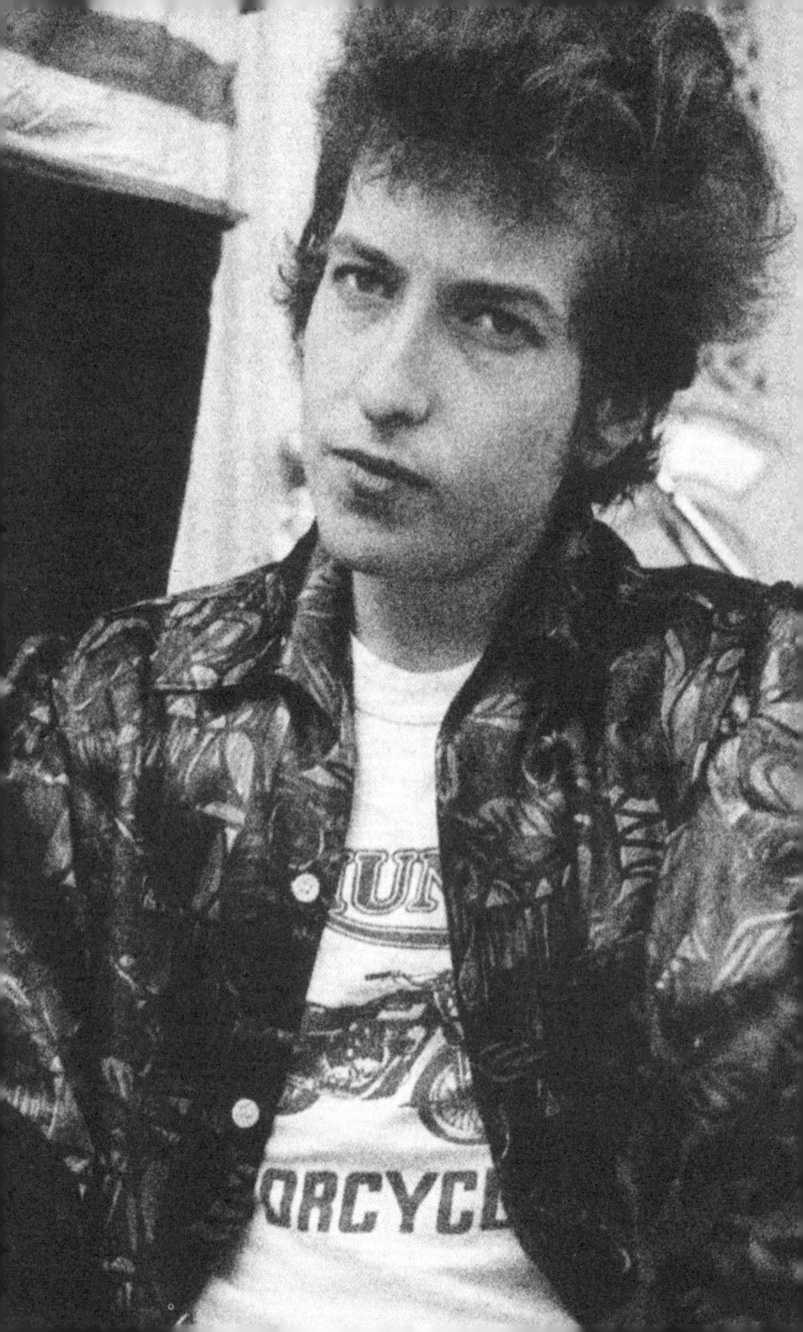

HIGHWAY 61 REVISITED
重访 61 号公路

像一块滚石

墓碑布鲁斯

要笑不容易,要哭只需坐火车

来自别克 6

瘦子的歌谣

准女王简

重访 61 号公路

恰似大拇指汤姆蓝调

荒芜巷

附加歌词

准是第四街 坐在带刺铁篱上
能不能请你从窗子爬出去?

1. Of war an peace/ the truth does twist/ it's curfew gull just glides/
upon the fungus forest cloud, the cowboy Angel rides
he lights his candle in the sun
An tho his candle burns the day it's glow is waxed in black
All ecpt when neath the trees of eden —

2. The lamppost stands with folded arms/ it's iron claws attached
t the curbs neath wailing babys — tho it's shadow's metal badge/
All in all, can only fall, with a crashing but meaningless blow
No sound comes from the depths of EDEN —

3. The SAVAGE SOLDIER sticks his head IN SAND An then complains
unto the shoeless hunter/who's grown deaf but still remains
upon the beach where hound dogs bay At ships with tattoed sails
heading for the gates of eden —

4. With his time rusted compass blade, ALLADIN An his LAMP
sits with utopian hermit monks SIDE SADDLE ON THE GOLDEN CALF
An on their promises of PARADISE, you will not hear a LAUGH
expt inside the gates of eden —

5. The motorcycle black MADONNA/ two wheeled GYPSY queen
to her silver studded phantom cause the grey flannel dwarf t scream
As he weeps t wicked birds of prey, who pick up his bread crumb sins
There are no sins once in the gates of eden —

6. relationships of ownership wait outside the wings (smile)
of those condemned fact accordingly waiting for succeeding kings
An I try t harmonize with songs/ the lonesome sparrow sings
All men are kings inside the gates of eden —

7. The Kingdoms of experience/ in the precious wind they rot
while paupers change possessions/each wishing for what the other's got
An the princess An the prince discuss what is real An what is not
It doesnt matter inside the gates of eden —

8. The foreign sun/ it rises/ oh A house that is not MINE
As friends An other strangers from their fates try to resign
Leaving men wholly total free t do anything they wish but die
There's no where t hide inside the gates of eden

9. At dawn my lover comes t me an tells me of her dreams

At times i think/there are no words, but these t tell
no truths,

《重访61号公路》是迪伦的第6张录音室专辑,由哥伦比亚唱片公司于1965年8月30日发行。除了11分钟的原声民谣《荒芜巷》,其他歌曲均为电声摇滚。一般认为,迪伦在这张专辑中以狂放的、游戏的、有时貌似疯言疯语的诗歌,配以强劲的电声布鲁斯,创作出了一批抓住了当时政治动荡和文化混乱神魂的歌曲。评论家迈克尔·格雷(Michael Gray)甚至认为:"从重要性上说,所谓的20世纪60年代,就是从这张专辑开始的。"

可以援引迪伦自传《编年史》(第一卷)中的一段话,帮助我们对这张专辑形成提纲挈领的认识:"61号公路,乡村布鲁斯的主干道,起始于我的家乡……准确地说是德卢斯。我经常觉得我是从它开始的,总是一直在它上面,从它那里可以去任何地方,甚至下到三角洲地区的腹心地带。这是相同的道路,充满了同样的矛盾、同样的小镇、同样的精神祖先。密西西比河,流着布鲁斯的血,也开始于我的家乡一带。我从来没有远离它的任何一处。它就是我在宇宙中的位置,我时常觉得它就在我的血液里。"(徐振锋、吴宏凯译)

1965年5月,迪伦从英国巡演归来身心俱疲,"我打算不再唱歌了。我已经筋疲力尽了。"出于不满,他写了篇20页长文,被他描述为"长长的呕吐物"。其后,他从中取出一部分,化为包含4段主歌和1段副歌的歌曲《像一块滚石》。创作这首歌扫去了他的厌恶感,恢复了他音乐创作的热情。近40年后再次回顾这段经历,迪伦说:"就像一个鬼魂在写这样一首歌……你不知道这意味着什么。"

以此开篇,《重访61号公路》的9首歌曲,为20世纪60年代定下了基调,其中6首歌都在5分半以上的长度。不同于一些艺人炫技性的布鲁斯,迪伦的长歌从来不是那种大段的乐器独奏,充塞其中的,是实实在在的长篇歌词。《像一块滚石》改变了商业规则和艺术惯例,打破了电台歌曲的长度限制,许多亲聆它的人都觉得被唤醒了,从不同方向感受到它的冲击和启示。

这张专辑用了两个录音室,从1965年6月15日到8月4日,将12首歌(有3首歌未被专辑收录)录了不下140遍。其间,在新港民谣音乐节上,迪伦因为"突变"而被大喝倒彩。专辑的大部分,都由新制作人鲍勃·约翰斯顿(Bob Johnston)监制完成。

《重访61号公路》成为迪伦第1张全摇滚专辑。此后,世界流行音乐的面貌为之一变,摇滚乐向着更文学、更奇幻、更聪明、更具探索性和更注重整体性的方向驶去。

专辑同名歌曲《重访61号公路》和《荒芜巷》《墓碑布鲁斯》《恰似大拇指汤姆蓝调》等极尽夸张胡搞之能事,有时像文学人物和历史名人的伪传记,有时像一幕接一幕的荒唐闹剧,有时像诡谲的魔幻奇观。总体来说,都是怪诞乱影,让人不由得联想和意会到现实的巨变、迷茫、荒诞和光怪陆离。《来自别克6》《准女王简》与《像一块滚石》，都反映了动荡时代无可挽回的失败，歌曲中的人物来自不同时代、不同地理和不同阶层，带着偏远的地方性，都有某种奇异光彩。《瘦子的歌谣》中更有诗歌史上最古怪的对话和"迪伦最伟大的原型人物"，体现了新兴反主流文化的离经叛道，为庸常世界所难解。整张专辑是怪人聚会，带着狂欢和喧闹的大冒险，用罗伯特·谢尔顿（Robert Shelton）的话说："我们的反英雄在疾病、绝望、妓女和圣人中间跌跌撞撞。"而讲述它们的，是一个嘶哑、嘲讽、神秘、苦乐难辨的声音，在电声器乐粗暴猛烈的攻击中半说半唱。

这里需要拎出为正统文化所不知晓的布鲁斯传统提醒一下各位，正如专辑名所示：无论文字还是音乐，这张专辑其实都是来自民间传统的再创造。《重访61号公路》是一部"歪曲的布鲁斯"。摇滚乐从音乐原型来说，其实就是电声布鲁斯。

《重访61号公路》被评论家称为"一部有凝聚力和概念性的作品""改变一切的专辑""开创性的民谣摇滚经典"。以可怕的、半生不熟的语言，丰富的、粗野的、喷薄而出的意象，它为更宽广深厚的摇滚乐开辟出了道路。所以有了日后那句著名断语："'猫王'解放了摇滚乐的身体，而迪伦解放了摇滚乐的灵魂。"

LIKE A ROLLING STONE

Once upon a time you dressed so fine
You threw the bums a dime in your prime, didn't you?
People'd call, say, "Beware doll, you're bound to fall"
You thought they were all kiddin' you
You used to laugh about
Everybody that was hangin' out
Now you don't talk so loud
Now you don't seem so proud
About having to be scrounging for your next meal

How does it feel
How does it feel
To be without a home
Like a complete unknown
Like a rolling stone?

You've gone to the finest school all right, Miss Lonely
But you know you only used to get juiced in it
And nobody has ever taught you how to live on the street
And now you find out you're gonna have to get used to it

像一块滚石 [1]

那会儿你衣着光鲜
丢块铜板给叫花子,正值春风得意,对吧?
人们喊:"当心姑娘,你会败落的"
你以为他们是在捉弄你
而常常嘲笑着
那些到处晃的家伙
现在你不再大声说话
现在你不再那么骄傲
不得不四处去蹭饭,为了下一顿温饱

这感觉如何
这感觉如何
从此无家可归
像一个彻底的无名氏
像一块滚石?

不错,你上过最好的学校,寂寞小姐
可你很清楚,你在那儿不过是三天两头地买醉
没人教你如何在大街上生活
现在你明白必须自己适应

---

[1] 本篇由郝佳校译。

You said you'd never compromise
With the mystery tramp, but now you realize
He's not selling any alibis
As you stare into the vacuum of his eyes
And ask him do you want to make a deal?

How does it feel
How does it feel
To be on your own
With no direction home
Like a complete unknown
Like a rolling stone?

You never turned around to see the frowns on the jugglers and the clowns
When they all come down and did tricks for you
You never understood that it ain't no good
You shouldn't let other people get your kicks for you
You used to ride on the chrome horse with your diplomat
Who carried on his shoulder a Siamese cat
Ain't it hard when you discover that
He really wasn't where it's at
After he took from you everything he could steal

How does it feel
How does it feel

你曾说永不妥协
与这些搞不懂的流浪汉,但现在你明白了
他不会为你做任何伪证
当你瞪着他眼中的虚空
问他"想不想与我做笔交易?"

这感觉如何
这感觉如何
孤单单一个人
没有家的去向
像一个彻底的无名氏
像一块滚石?

你从不回身看看,魔术师和小丑的
　皱眉
当他们全走过来给你变戏法
你从不明白,这并非什么好事
你不该拿别人来寻开心
那时你跟你的外交家,常一起骑着枣红马
他肩上还蜷着一只暹罗猫
这是不是很难受当你发现
他完完全全变了个人
在偷光了你一切能偷的东西之后

这感觉如何
这感觉如何

To be on your own

With no direction home

Like a complete unknown

Like a rolling stone?

Princess on the steeple and all the pretty people

They're drinkin', thinkin' that they got it made

Exchanging all kinds of precious gifts and things

But you'd better lift your diamond ring, you'd better pawn it babe

You used to be so amused

At Napoleon in rags and the language that he used

Go to him now, he calls you, you can't refuse

When you got nothing, you got nothing to lose

You're invisible now, you got no secrets to conceal

How does it feel

How does it feel

To be on your own

With no direction home

Like a complete unknown

Like a rolling stone?

孤单单一个人
没有家的去向
像一个彻底的无名氏
像一块滚石?

尖塔上的公主,所有的漂亮人儿
他们喝着酒,想着一切皆为其所设
而彼此交换着各种珍贵礼物
但你最好摘下钻戒,最好把它送去
　典当
小妞,过去你总是取笑
拿破仑的破衣烂衫,还有他的谈吐
但是去找他吧,他在叫你,你无法拒绝
现在你什么都没有,什么也不会失去
你是看不见的人,已没有秘密要隐藏

这感觉如何
这感觉如何
孤单单一个人
没有家的去向
像一个彻底的无名氏
像一块滚石?

TOMBSTONE BLUES

The sweet pretty things are in bed now of course
The city fathers they're trying to endorse
The reincarnation of Paul Revere's horse
But the town has no need to be nervous

The ghost of Belle Starr she hands down her wits
To Jezebel the nun she violently knits
A bald wig for Jack the Ripper who sits
At the head of the chamber of commerce

Mama's in the fact'ry
She ain't got no shoes
Daddy's in the alley
He's lookin' for the fuse
I'm in the streets
With the tombstone blues

墓碑布鲁斯

当然这时候,可爱的尤物们早睡了
市里的大人物还在忙着签字
批准保罗·里维尔的坐骑[1]转世
但是城市大可不必焦虑

贝尔·斯塔尔[2]的魂儿
把智慧传给修女耶洗别,修女
猛力编织秃顶假发给开膛手杰克[3]
杰克坐在商会的头把椅子上

妈妈在工厂里
没有鞋子
爸爸在巷子里
找着保险丝
我在大街上
弄这墓碑布鲁斯

---

[1] 保罗·里维尔的马,美国独立战争第一仗,英军计划突袭,银匠保罗·里维尔策马去报信,告知独立军。
[2] 贝尔·斯塔尔(1848—1889),美国西部女匪,有"强盗女王"之称。
[3] 19世纪以残忍手法连续杀害多名妓女的伦敦杀人犯,始终逍遥法外。

The hysterical bride in the penny arcade
Screaming she moans, "I've just been made"
Then sends out for the doctor who pulls down the shade
Says, "My advice is to not let the boys in"

Now the medicine man comes and he shuffles inside
He walks with a swagger and he says to the bride
"Stop all this weeping, swallow your pride
You will not die, it's not poison"

Mama's in the fact'ry
She ain't got no shoes
Daddy's in the alley
He's lookin' for the fuse
I'm in the streets
With the tombstone blues

Well, John the Baptist after torturing a thief
Looks up at his hero the Commander-in-Chief
Saying, "Tell me great hero, but please make it brief
Is there a hole for me to get sick in?"

The Commander-in-Chief answers him while chasing a fly
Saying, "Death to all those who would whimper and cry"

平价集市里歇斯底里的新娘
尖叫着呻吟:"我刚刚被骗了"
然后派人请医生,医生拉下卷帘
说:"我建议不要让男生进来"

这时巫医到了,他拖着脚
大摇大摆地进来,对新娘说道
"别哭了,吞下你的骄傲
你不会死,这不是毒药"

妈妈在工厂里
没有鞋子
爸爸在巷子里
找着保险丝
我在大街上
弄这墓碑布鲁斯

哦,施洗者约翰[1]折磨完了小偷
抬头看他的英雄总司令
说:"告诉我大英雄,但请扼要简明
有没有坑,能让我吐一吐?"

总司令一边追苍蝇,一边回答
"哭哭啼啼的家伙都去死吧"

---

[1] 施洗者约翰,指受神差遣为耶稣施以洗礼的人。

And dropping a barbell he points to the sky
Saying, "The sun's not yellow it's chicken"

Mama's in the fact'ry
She ain't got no shoes
Daddy's in the alley
He's lookin' for the fuse
I'm in the streets
With the tombstone blues

The king of the Philistines his soldiers to save
Puts jawbones on their tombstones and flatters their graves
Puts the pied pipers in prison and fattens the slaves
Then sends them out to the jungle

Gypsy Davey with a blowtorch he burns out their camps
With his faithful slave Pedro behind him he tramps
With a fantastic collection of stamps
To win friends and influence his uncle

Mama's in the fact'ry
She ain't got no shoes
Daddy's in the alley

然后他扔下杠铃,手指天空
说:"太阳不黄,是鸡肉[1]"

妈妈在工厂里
没有鞋子
爸爸在巷子里
找着保险丝
我在大街上
弄这墓碑布鲁斯

非利士人[2]的王要救他的兵
把下颌骨们放在碑上,美化他们的坟
将花衣笛手们投进监狱,养肥了奴隶
然后送他们去丛林

吉卜赛人戴维,用喷灯烧掉了营地
忠实的奴隶佩德罗,跟着他跋山涉水
收集了好得不得了的邮票
拿它四处结交,影响他的叔叔

妈妈在工厂里
没有鞋子
爸爸在巷子里

---

[1] 鸡肉,俚语中有"胆小鬼"之意。
[2] 非利士人,喻指庸人、市侩。

He's lookin' for the fuse
I'm in the streets
With the tombstone blues

The geometry of innocence flesh on the bone
Causes Galileo's math book to get thrown
At Delilah who sits worthlessly alone
But the tears on her cheeks are from laughter

Now I wish I could give Brother Bill his great thrill
I would set him in chains at the top of the hill
Then send out for some pillars and Cecil B. DeMille
He could die happily ever after

Mama's in the fact'ry
She ain't got no shoes
Daddy's in the alley
He's lookin' for the fuse
I'm in the streets
With the tombstone blues

Where Ma Rainey and Beethoven once unwrapped their bedroll

找着保险丝
我在大街上
弄这墓碑布鲁斯

天真之几何得以充实
致使伽利略的数学书,扔给了
大利拉 [1],她一文不值,一个人坐着
脸上的泪水却来自欢笑

说到这,我希望能给比尔修士惊喜
我会把他用铁链锁在山巅
再去找几根柱子,加上塞西尔·B. 德米尔 [2]
他会幸福地死去直到永远

妈妈在工厂里
没有鞋子
爸爸在巷子里
找着保险丝
我在大街上
弄这墓碑布鲁斯

雷妮妈妈 [3] 和贝多芬卷起铺盖的地方

---

[1] 大利拉,参孙所爱之人,后经非利士人利诱,出卖了参孙。
[2] 塞西尔·B. 德米尔,美国电影导演,执导过《参孙与大利拉》。
[3] 雷妮妈妈,即玛·雷尼,美国歌手,有"蓝调之母"之誉。

Tuba players now rehearse around the flagpole
And the National Bank at a profit sells road maps for the soul
To the old folks home and the college

Now I wish I could write you a melody so plain
That could hold you dear lady from going insane
That could ease you and cool you and cease the pain
Of your useless and pointless knowledge

Mama's in the fact'ry
She ain't got no shoes
Daddy's in the alley
He's lookin' for the fuse
I'm in the streets
With the tombstone blues

现在大号手们围着旗杆在排练
而国家银行为了赚钱,在卖灵魂路线图
给大学和养老院

说到这,我多希望给你写段平实无比的旋律
可以保护你亲爱的女士,不至于犯精神病
可以让你放松让你冷静
祛除你无用又无谓的知识导致的苦痛

妈妈在工厂里
没有鞋子
爸爸在巷子里
找着保险丝
我在大街上
弄这墓碑布鲁斯

IT TAKES A LOT TO LAUGH, IT TAKES A TRAIN TO CRY

Well, I ride on a mailtrain, baby
Can't buy a thrill
Well, I've been up all night, baby
Leanin' on the windowsill
Well, if I die
On top of the hill
And if I don't make it
You know my baby will

Don't the moon look good, mama
Shinin' through the trees?
Don't the brakeman look good, mama
Flagging down the "Double E"?
Don't the sun look good
Goin' down over the sea?
Don't my gal look fine
When she's comin' after me?

要笑不容易，
要哭只需坐火车 [1]

唉，我乘坐着邮车，宝贝
买不来刺激
唉，我整宿都没睡，宝贝
斜倚着那窗子
唉，如果我死了
死在那山顶
这事儿我没搞定
你知道我的宝贝会搞定

月亮看上去不美吗？妈妈 [2]
它穿过枝丫闪烁
制动员看上去不美吗？妈妈
他摇号旗拦下"双 E"车
太阳看上去不美吗？妈妈
它在海平面上沉落
我的妞看上去不美吗？
当她在我后面跟着

---

[1] 本篇由杨盈盈校译。
[2] 妈妈，美国俚语对情人的称呼。

Now the wintertime is coming
The windows are filled with frost
I went to tell everybody
But I could not get across
Well, I wanna be your lover, baby
I don't wanna be your boss
Don't say I never warned you
When your train gets lost

眼下冬时将至
窗上结满寒霜
我去通知每个人
却没有办法过去
唉,我要做你情人,宝贝
我不想做你上司
别说我没警告你
在你的火车迷路时

FROM A BUICK 6

I got this graveyard woman, you know she keeps my kid
But my soulful mama, you know she keeps me hid
She's a junkyard angel and she always gives me bread
Well, if I go down dyin', you know she bound to put a blanket on my bed

Well, when the pipeline gets broken and I'm lost on the river bridge
I'm cracked up on the highway and on the water's edge
She comes down the thruway ready to sew me up with thread
Well, if I go down dyin', you know she bound to put a blanket on my bed

Well, she don't make me nervous, she don't talk too much
She walks like Bo Diddley and she don't need no crutch
She keeps this four-ten all loaded with lead
Well, if I go down dyin', you know she bound to put a blanket on my bed

来自别克 6 [1]

我有个看墓地的女人,你知道她养着我的孩子
但我情深似海的妈妈 [2] 呀,你知道她还帮着我藏身
她是垃圾场天使,总是给我面包吃
唉,如果我要死了,你知道她一准为我铺好
　　毯子

唉,当油管爆了而我在跨河大桥又
　　迷了路
我一头撞上了公路一头撞上了河堤
她从公路跑下来要用针线把我缝起来
唉,如果我要死了,你知道她一准为我铺好
　　毯子

唉,她不让我紧张,她话不多
走路像博·迪德利,而且她不需要拐杖
她给这把四一〇 [3] 总是上满了铅弹
唉,如果我要死了,你知道她一准为我铺好
　　毯子

---

[1] 别克 6,别克公司 1914—1930 年间生产的一款汽车。
[2] 妈妈,美国俚语中对情人的称呼。
[3] 四一〇,口径为 0.410 英寸的枪。

Well, you know I need a steam shovel mama to keep away the dead
I need a dump truck mama to unload my head
She brings me everything and more, and just like I said
Well, if I go down dyin', you know she bound to put a blanket on my bed

唉,妈妈,你知道我需要一台蒸汽铲来
　　铲死人
妈妈我需要一辆自卸卡车卸我的脑袋
她会把所有东西带来,比所有更多,就像我说的
唉,如果我要死了,你知道她一准为我铺好
　　毯子

BALLAD OF A THIN MAN

You walk into the room
With your pencil in your hand
You see somebody naked
And you say, "Who is that man?"
You try so hard
But you don't understand
Just what you'll say
When you get home

Because something is happening here
But you don't know what it is
Do you, Mister Jones?

You raise up your head
And you ask, "Is this where it is?"
And somebody points to you and says
"It's his"
And you say, "What's mine?"
And somebody else says, "Where what is?"
And you say, "Oh my God
Am I here all alone?"

瘦子的歌谣

你走进房间
手拿着铅笔
你看见一人一丝不挂
于是问:"那人是谁?"
你那么努力
可还是搞不明白
回到家以后
该说什么

因为这里正有事发生
可你不知道是什么
是吧,琼斯先生?

你抬起头
于是问:"就这儿?"
有人指着你说
"是他的"
于是你说:"我的什么?"
又一人说:"什么在哪?"
于是你说:"啊我的上帝
这儿就我一人吗?"

Because something is happening here
But you don't know what it is
Do you, Mister Jones?

You hand in your ticket
And you go watch the geek
Who immediately walks up to you
When he hears you speak
And says, "How does it feel
To be such a freak?"
And you say, "Impossible"
As he hands you a bone

Because something is happening here
But you don't know what it is
Do you, Mister Jones?

You have many contacts
Among the lumberjacks
To get you facts
When someone attacks your imagination
But nobody has any respect
Anyway they already expect you
To just give a check
To tax-deductible charity organizations

因为这里正有事发生
可你不知道是什么
是吧,琼斯先生?

你递上了门票
要看怪胎展
怪胎听见你说话
立马朝你走过来
说:"作为怪物
是什么感觉?"
于是你说:"不可能"
而他递给你一根骨头

因为这里正有事发生
可你不知道是什么
是吧,琼斯先生?

伐木工人中间
有你的许多熟人
给你提供事实
当有人攻击你的想象力
然而没人尊重你
不管怎样他们寄希望你
开一张支票
给减税的慈善组织

You've been with the professors
And they've all liked your looks
With great lawyers you have
Discussed lepers and crooks
You've been through all of
F. Scott Fitzgerald's books
You're very well read
It's well known

Because something is happening here
But you don't know what it is
Do you, Mister Jones?

Well, the sword swallower, he comes up to you
And then he kneels
He crosses himself
And then he clicks his high heels
And without further notice
He asks you how it feels
And he says, "Here is your throat back
Thanks for the loan"

Because something is happening here
But you don't know what it is
Do you, Mister Jones?

你和教授们有交往
他们都喜欢你的长相
你和大律师们讨论过
麻风病人和骗子
你通读过
F. 斯科特·菲茨杰拉德的著作
你博览群书
世人皆知

因为这里正有事发生
可你不知道是什么
是吧,琼斯先生?

哦,吞剑人朝你走来
然后他跪下了
刺穿了自己
然后他踩响了高跟鞋
并无另行通知
他问你感觉如何
然后他说:"你的喉咙还给你
谢谢你借我"

因为这里正有事发生
可你不知道是什么
是吧,琼斯先生?

Now you see this one-eyed midget
Shouting the word "NOW"
And you say, "For what reason?"
And he says, "How?"
And you say, "What does this mean?"
And he screams back, "You're a cow
Give me some milk
Or else go home"

Because something is happening here
But you don't know what it is
Do you, Mister Jones?

Well, you walk into the room
Like a camel and then you frown
You put your eyes in your pocket
And your nose on the ground
There ought to be a law
Against you comin' around
You should be made
To wear earphones

Because something is happening here
But you don't know what it is
Do you, Mister Jones?

现在你看到这个独眼侏儒了
他在喊着"现在"这个词
于是你说："因为什么？"
然后他说："如何？"
于是你说："这什么意思？"
然后他尖叫着回道："你这头母牛
给我奶
不然就滚回家去"

因为这里正有事发生
可你不知道是什么
是吧，琼斯先生？

哦，你走进房间
像头骆驼一样，然后你皱眉
把眼睛放进口袋
把鼻子搁在地上
真该有条法规
禁止你到处晃
你该被勒令
戴上耳机

因为这里正有事发生
可你不知道是什么
是吧，琼斯先生？

QUEEN JANE APPROXIMATELY

When your mother sends back all your invitations
And your father to your sister he explains
That you're tired of yourself and all of your creations
Won't you come see me, Queen Jane?
Won't you come see me, Queen Jane?

Now when all of the flower ladies want back what they have lent you
And the smell of their roses does not remain
And all of your children start to resent you
Won't you come see me, Queen Jane?
Won't you come see me, Queen Jane?

Now when all the clowns that you have commissioned
Have died in battle or in vain
And you're sick of all this repetition
Won't you come see me, Queen Jane?
Won't you come see me, Queen Jane?

准女王简 [1]

当母亲退回你所有的请帖
而父亲跟你姐姐解释
说你厌倦了自己和你的所有作品
你不来看我吗,简女王?
你不来看我吗,简女王?

如今,当所有的花夫人都索回了借你的
　物品
而她们的玫瑰花香已经散尽
而你所有的孩子都开始怨恨你
你不来看我吗,简女王?
你不来看我吗,简女王?

如今,当你雇佣来的所有小丑
都已战死沙场或死得一文不值
而你厌倦了所有这些反反复复
你不来看我吗,简女王?
你不来看我吗,简女王?

---

[1] 简·格雷(Lady Jane Grey, 1537—1554),在位只有9天即被废黜的英女王,一般不正式算作英国女王。

When all of your advisers heave their plastic
At your feet to convince you of your pain
Trying to prove that your conclusions should be more drastic
Won't you come see me, Queen Jane?
Won't you come see me, Queen Jane?

Now when all the bandits that you turned your other cheek to
All lay down their bandanas and complain
And you want somebody you don't have to speak to
Won't you come see me, Queen Jane?
Won't you come see me, Queen Jane?

当你所有的顾问都将他们的塑料
抛掷在你脚下,以让你确信自己的痛苦
试图证明你的决定理应更激进
你不来看我吗,简女王?
你不来看我吗,简女王?

如今,当你转过另一边脸去对待的强盗 [1]
全扯下了头巾发牢骚
而你想找个你不必与之交谈的人
你不来看我吗,简女王?
你不来看我吗,简女王?

---

[1] 《新约·马太福音》5:39:"只是我告诉你们:不要与恶人作对。有人打你的右脸,连左脸也转过来由他打。"

HIGHWAY 61 REVISITED

Oh God said to Abraham, "Kill me a son"
Abe says, "Man, you must be puttin' me on"
God say, "No." Abe say, "What?"
God say, "You can do what you want Abe, but
The next time you see me comin' you better run"
Well Abe says, "Where do you want this killin' done?"
God says, "Out on Highway 61"

Well Georgia Sam he had a bloody nose
Welfare Department they wouldn't give him no clothes
He asked poor Howard where can I go
Howard said there's only one place I know
Sam said tell me quick man I got to run
Ol' Howard just pointed with his gun
And said that way down on Highway 61

Well Mack the Finger said to Louie the King
I got forty red white and blue shoestrings

重访 61 号公路 [1]

哦上帝对亚伯拉罕说:"给我宰个儿子"
亚伯说:"老兄,你一准是要我"
上帝说:"不是。"亚伯说:"什么?"
上帝说:"想怎么着怎么着吧亚伯
但下次,你看到我最好快跑"
于是亚伯说:"你想在哪儿宰?"
上帝说:"去 61 号公路"

哦乔治亚·萨姆流鼻血了
福利部不肯给他衣服
他问穷汉霍华德,我能到哪儿去
霍华德说我只知道一个地方
萨姆说快说老兄我得赶紧走
老霍华德只是用枪一指
说那边,顺着 61 号公路

哦"指头麦克"对路易国王说
我有四十根红白蓝鞋带儿

---

[1] 61 号公路,连接着迪伦的出生地明尼苏达州德卢斯与布鲁斯"摇篮"密西西比三角洲的一条路,其间穿过圣路易斯、孟菲斯、新奥尔良等布鲁斯重镇,有"布鲁斯公路"之称。

And a thousand telephones that don't ring

Do you know where I can get rid of these things

And Louie the King said let me think for a minute son

And he said yes I think it can be easily done

Just take everything down to Highway 61

Now the fifth daughter on the twelfth night

Told the first father that things weren't right

My complexion she said is much too white

He said come here and step into the light he says hmm you're
   right

Let me tell the second mother this has been done

But the second mother was with the seventh son

And they were both out on Highway 61

Now the rovin' gambler he was very bored

He was tryin' to create a next world war

He found a promoter who nearly fell off the floor

He said I never engaged in this kind of thing before

But yes I think it can be very easily done

We'll just put some bleachers out in the sun

And have it on Highway 61

还有一千台不响的电话机
你说我在哪儿能处理掉这些玩意儿
路易国王说让我想一下孩子
然后说有了我想这事儿好办
把它们统统拿到 61 号公路

这会儿第五个闺女在第十二夜
告诉第一个父亲不好了
说我的肤色太白了
他说过来站到光里,他说嗯你是
  对的
让我告诉二妈这事儿成了
但是二妈正带着第七个儿子
两人都去了 61 号公路

这会儿那流浪赌徒觉得无聊
他想制造下一次世界大战
他找到一个差点儿摔地上的发起人
发起人说我以前没弄过这个
不过有了我想这事儿很好办
我们只消在太阳底下弄些露天看台
就在 61 号公路

JUST LIKE TOM THUMB'S BLUES

When you're lost in the rain in Juarez

And it's Eastertime too

And your gravity fails

And negativity don't pull you through

Don't put on any airs

When you're down on Rue Morgue Avenue

They got some hungry women there

And they really make a mess outa you

Now if you see Saint Annie

Please tell her thanks a lot

I cannot move

My fingers are all in a knot

I don't have the strength

To get up and take another shot

And my best friend, my doctor

Won't even say what it is I've got

Sweet Melinda

恰似大拇指汤姆[1]蓝调

当你迷失在华雷斯的雨中
适逢复活节
你又在失重
负能量也不能把你拽出来
别摆架子了
当你走在莫格街
那儿有一些饥渴女人
着实把你搞得灰头土脸

好,若你见到圣安妮[2]
请代我向她致谢
我动弹不了
手指都打了结
没有力气
爬起来再来一次
而且我最好的朋友,我的医生
甚至都不告诉我得了什么病

甜姐梅琳达

---

[1] 大拇指汤姆,即拇指男孩,《格林童话》中身体只有拇指大的男孩。
[2] 圣安妮,未见于《圣经》,但民间传统认为她是圣母玛利亚之母。

The peasants call her the goddess of gloom
She speaks good English
And she invites you up into her room
And you're so kind
And careful not to go to her too soon
And she takes your voice
And leaves you howling at the moon

Up on Housing Project Hill
It's either fortune or fame
You must pick up one or the other
Though neither of them are to be what they claim
If you're lookin' to get silly
You better go back to from where you came
Because the cops don't need you
And man they expect the same

Now all the authorities
They just stand around and boast
How they blackmailed the sergeant-at-arms
Into leaving his post
And picking up Angel who
Just arrived here from the coast
Who looked so fine at first
But left looking just like a ghost

农民们都叫她忧郁女神
她英语说得好
她请你去她房里
而你真是好心
特意没去得太早
但她拿走了你的嗓音
留下你对着月亮嚎叫

在"安居工程山"上
要么财富要么名望
你不选这就得选那
尽管两者都不是它们声称的那样
如果你想犯傻
最好原路返回
因为警察不需要你
也希望你老兄不需要他们

这会儿所有的当权者
都只是站在那儿吹牛
吹他们如何敲诈监察官
逼迫他离开了岗位
开车子去接
刚从海边抵达的"天使"
"天使"起先貌美无比
离开时却恍如鬼魅

I started out on burgundy

But soon hit the harder stuff

Everybody said they'd stand behind me

When the game got rough

But the joke was on me

There was nobody even there to call my bluff

I'm going back to New York City

I do believe I've had enough

我开始喝勃艮第
但很快碰了那些烈性玩意儿
每个人都说等事情变糟时
他会在背后撑我
可当我成了笑话
连个要我摊牌的人都没了
我要回纽约
我想我已经够了

DESOLATION ROW

They're selling postcards of the hanging
They're painting the passports brown
The beauty parlor is filled with sailors
The circus is in town
Here comes the blind commissioner
They've got him in a trance
One hand is tied to the tight-rope walker
The other is in his pants
And the riot squad they're restless
They need somewhere to go
As Lady and I look out tonight
From Desolation Row

Cinderella, she seems so easy
"It takes one to know one," she smiles
And puts her hands in her back pockets
Bette Davis style

荒芜巷

他们在贩卖绞刑明信片
他们在把护照涂成棕黄 [1]
美容院里挤满水手
马戏团来到镇上
这边厢盲警长驾到
眼前的一切让他恍惚
他一只手绑在走钢丝人的身上
另一只手伸进裤子
而防暴队焦躁不安
他们有地方需要赶过去
是夜,"女士"和我向外张望
从荒芜巷

灰姑娘,她看上去特轻松
"彼此彼此"她微笑着
把两手插进后面的口袋
一副贝蒂·戴维斯 [2] 的造型

---

[1] "把护照涂成棕黄",美国行政官员因公护照为棕黄色,不同于一般护照的蓝色。
[2] 贝蒂·戴维斯(Bette Davis,1908—1989),美国电影明星,把手插在后衣口袋是她在电影中的一个造型。

And in comes Romeo, he's moaning

"You Belong to Me I Believe"

And someone says, "You're in the wrong place my friend

You better leave"

And the only sound that's left

After the ambulances go

Is Cinderella sweeping up

On Desolation Row

Now the moon is almost hidden

The stars are beginning to hide

The fortune-telling lady

Has even taken all her things inside

All except for Cain and Abel

And the hunchback of Notre Dame

Everybody is making love

Or else expecting rain

And the Good Samaritan, he's dressing

He's getting ready for the show

He's going to the carnival tonight

On Desolation Row

那边厢罗密欧进来了,呻吟般唱着
《我相信你属于我》[1]
有人说:"你来错地儿了朋友
最好出去"
最后,剩下的唯一声音
在救护车走后
是灰姑娘在扫地
在荒芜巷

这会儿月亮几乎没影了
星星开始躲起来
算命婆
甚至把她的东西也都收拾了
所有人,除了该隐和亚伯
还有《巴黎圣母院》的驼背敲钟人
大家都在做爱
要不就等着下雨
而那个好撒玛利亚人[2],正在穿戴
在为演出做准备
今晚他将出席嘉年华
在荒芜巷

---

[1] 歌曲名,本诗后面出现的加书名号的作品名中有的确有其曲,有的近似歌名的歌曲为迪伦杜撰。
[2] "好撒玛利亚人",意为好心人、见义勇为者。

Now Ophelia, she's 'neath the window
For her I feel so afraid
On her twenty-second birthday
She already is an old maid
To her, death is quite romantic
She wears an iron vest
Her profession's her religion
Her sin is her lifelessness
And though her eyes are fixed upon
Noah's great rainbow
She spends her time peeking
Into Desolation Row

Einstein, disguised as Robin Hood
With his memories in a trunk
Passed this way an hour ago
With his friend, a jealous monk
He looked so immaculately frightful
As he bummed a cigarette
Then he went off sniffing drainpipes
And reciting the alphabet
Now you would not think to look at him

这会儿奥菲利娅[1]，在窗户下面
我非常担心她
在二十二岁生日这天
她已经成了老姑娘
对她而言，死亡相当浪漫
她穿一件铁背心
她的宗教就是她的职业
她的罪过是她的死气沉沉
虽然两眼紧盯着
挪亚的大彩虹[2]
她也花时间偷看
那荒芜巷

爱因斯坦，装扮成罗宾汉
拎着装满他记忆的大箱子
一小时前刚路过这里
和他的朋友，一个嫉妒的僧侣
他的样子真令人毛骨悚然
他向路人讨了支烟
又跑去嗅排水管
一边还背着字母表
你现在不想看他了

---

[1] 莎士比亚《哈姆雷特》中的女主角，哈姆雷特的未婚妻，因发疯溺水而死。
[2] 上帝以彩虹为记，与挪亚立约不再发大洪水毁灭世界。

But he was famous long ago
For playing the electric violin
On Desolation Row

Dr. Filth, he keeps his world
Inside of a leather cup
But all his sexless patients
They're trying to blow it up
Now his nurse, some local loser
She's in charge of the cyanide hole
And she also keeps the cards that read
"Have Mercy on His Soul"
They all play on pennywhistles
You can hear them blow
If you lean your head out far enough
From Desolation Row

Across the street they've nailed the curtains
They're getting ready for the feast
The Phantom of the Opera
A perfect image of a priest
They're spoonfeeding Casanova
To get him to feel more assured

可当年他真是家喻户晓
就为表演带电的小提琴
在荒芜巷

污秽医生，把他的世界
存放在一只皮杯里
而他所有的无性病人
都想把它给炸了
这会儿他的护士，一位当地的废物
负责掌管着氰化室
也保管着那些卡片，上面写着
《垂怜他的灵魂》
他们都吹六孔小竖笛
你能听到他们的笛音
只要把脑袋探得够远
从荒芜巷

街对面他们钉死了窗帘
准备着盛宴
《歌剧魅影》[1]
一幅完美的祭司形象
他们一勺勺喂着卡萨诺瓦[2]
好让他更放心

---

[1] 英国作曲家安德鲁·韦伯的著名音乐剧。
[2] 卡萨诺瓦（1725—1798），意大利冒险家、作家，"情圣"。

Then they'll kill him with self-confidence
After poisoning him with words
And the Phantom's shouting to skinny girls
"Get Outa Here If You Don't Know
Casanova is just being punished for going
To Desolation Row"

Now at midnight all the agents
And the superhuman crew
Come out and round up everyone
That knows more than they do
Then they bring them to the factory
Where the heart-attack machine
Is strapped across their shoulders
And then the kerosene
Is brought down from the castles
By insurance men who go
Check to see that nobody is escaping
To Desolation Row

Praise be to Nero's Neptune
The Titanic sails at dawn
And everybody's shouting
"Which Side Are You On?"

然后即用自信杀死他
在以语言给他下毒之后
而"魅影"在对皮包骨的姑娘们高唱
《离开这里,如果你们不知道》
卡萨诺瓦在受惩罚,只因为他
去了荒芜巷"

这会儿是午夜,所有的特工
所有的超人队员,全部出动
把知道得比他们多的人
统统抓起来
随后把他们带到工厂
在那儿把心脏病发作机
绑在他们肩膀上
然后煤油
从城堡运下来,运送者
都是保险业务员,他们
四下查检,确保没有人逃脱
去了荒芜巷

荣耀归于尼禄的海王星
泰坦尼克号在黎明启程
每个人都在喊
《你站哪一边?》

And Ezra Pound and T. S. Eliot
Fighting in the captain's tower
While calypso singers laugh at them
And fishermen hold flowers
Between the windows of the sea
Where lovely mermaids flow
And nobody has to think too much
About Desolation Row

Yes, I received your letter yesterday
(About the time the doorknob broke)
When you asked how I was doing
Was that some kind of joke?
All these people that you mention
Yes, I know them, they're quite lame
I had to rearrange their faces
And give them all another name
Right now I can't read too good
Don't send me no more letters no
Not unless you mail them
From Desolation Row

埃兹拉·庞德和 T. S. 艾略特 [1]
在船长塔里对打
一边是卡利普索歌手在讥笑他们
一边是渔民们手捧鲜花
在大海的两扇窗之间
可爱的美人鱼来回漂游
而没有人需要思考太多
关于荒芜巷

是的，我昨天收到了信
（大概是门把手坏掉的时候）
你问我过得如何
你是在开玩笑吧？
你提到的这些人
没错，我都认识，尽是蹩脚货
我不得不重新组装他们的脸
再给他们都重新取名
此刻我阅读有点儿障碍
不要再给我寄信了，不要了
除非你寄的信
发自荒芜巷

---

[1] 20 世纪英美两位大诗人，曾一起创作，私交甚笃。

POSITIVELY 4TH STREET

You got a lotta nerve
To say you are my friend
When I was down
You just stood there grinning

You got a lotta nerve
To say you got a helping hand to lend
You just want to be on
The side that's winning

You say I let you down
You know it's not like that
If you're so hurt
Why then don't you show it

You say you lost your faith
But that's not where it's at
You had no faith to lose

准是第四街[1]

你胆儿真大
声称是我朋友
我倒霉那会儿
你只站那儿咧嘴

你胆儿真大
说你会去拉一把
你不过是想
站在胜者一边儿

你说我让你失望了
你知道才不是那样
如果你很受伤
何不表现出来

你说你失去了信仰
但这也是个假把戏
你并无信仰可失

---

[1] 迪伦刚到纽约那段时间曾住在纽约第四街,那里是当时民谣运动的中心。这首歌大体反映了他与最初那帮老朋友、民谣圈子、左翼知识分子阵营的分道扬镳。

And you know it

I know the reason
That you talk behind my back
I used to be among the crowd
You're in with

Do you take me for such a fool
To think I'd make contact
With the one who tries to hide
What he don't know to begin with

You see me on the street
You always act surprised
You say, "How are you?" "Good luck"
But you don't mean it

When you know as well as me
You'd rather see me paralyzed
Why don't you just come out once
And scream it

No, I do not feel that good
When I see the heartbreaks you embrace
If I was a master thief
Perhaps I'd rob them

这你知道得清清楚楚

我知道为什么
你在背后说我坏话
因为我和你是一伙
但现在不是了

你当我是傻瓜吗
会和你这种人联系
一个试图藏匿
他不知道的东西的人

每回在街上碰见
你总是装作很惊讶
你说:"还好吗?""祝好运"
你可真会演戏

你和我一样清楚
你宁愿看到我瘫痪
何不直接跳出来
大声说它一次

不,我的感觉并不好
当我看到你拥抱那些心碎
如果我是个神偷
说不定会把它们抢走

And now I know you're dissatisfied
With your position and your place
Don't you understand
It's not my problem

I wish that for just one time
You could stand inside my shoes
And just for that one moment
I could be you

Yes, I wish that for just one time
You could stand inside my shoes
You'd know what a drag it is
To see you

当然现在我明白了
你对你的地位和立场不满意
难道你就不明白
这不是我的问题

我只希望能有一次
你站在我的鞋子里
而就在那一刻
我变成了你

是的,我只希望能有一次
你站在我的鞋子里
那样你就会知道,见到你
是怎样的腻味透顶

CAN YOU PLEASE CRAWL OUT YOUR WINDOW?

He sits in your room, his tomb, with a fist full of tacks
Preoccupied with his vengeance
Cursing the dead that can't answer him back
I'm sure that he has no intentions
Of looking your way, unless it's to say
That he needs you to test his inventions

Can you please crawl out your window?
Use your arms and legs it won't ruin you
How can you say he will haunt you?
You can go back to him any time you want to

He looks so truthful, is this how he feels
Trying to peel the moon and expose it
With his businesslike anger and his bloodhounds that kneel
If he needs a third eye he just grows it
He just needs you to talk or to hand him his chalk
Or pick it up after he throws it

Can you please crawl out your window?
Use your arms and legs it won't ruin you
How can you say he will haunt you?

能不能请你从窗子爬出去?

他坐在你房间,他的墓室里,满是想法
一心想着要复仇
诅咒着已不会答话的逝者
我敢肯定他一眼都不想
看向你,除非
他需要你验证他的假设

能不能请你从窗子爬出去?
动动胳膊腿儿不会毁了你
你怎能说你被他阴魂缠身?
你随时可以找他只要你想回去

他看起来如此真诚,他是这么想的吗
要剥下月亮的皮示众
以公事公办的愤怒和他寻血猎犬,跪着的?
如果他需要第三只眼,他就会长出它
他只是需要你跟他说话,给他递粉笔
或在他扔掉后再帮他捡起

能不能请你从窗子爬出去?
动动胳膊腿儿不会毁了你
你怎能说你被他阴魂缠身?

You can go back to him any time you want to

Why does he look so righteous while your face is so changed
Are you frightened of the box you keep him in
While his genocide fools and his friends rearrange
Their religion of the little tin women
That backs up their views but your face is so bruised
Come on out the dark is beginning

Can you please crawl out your window?
Use your arms and legs it won't ruin you
How can you say he will haunt you?
You can go back to him any time you want to

你随时可以找他只要你想回去

为何他看起来那么正直但你脸色大变
你就那么害怕那只装他的盒子？
当他那帮种族灭绝的白痴和伙伴
重整对小锡女的信仰
以支持他们的观点，可你鼻青脸肿
都快出来吧，黑暗开始了

能不能请你从窗子爬出去？
动动胳膊腿儿不会毁了你
你怎能说你被他阴魂缠身？
你随时可以找他只要你想回去

SITTING ON A BARBED-WIRE FENCE

I paid fifteen million dollars, twelve hundred and seventy-two cents
I paid one thousand two hundred twenty-seven dollars and fifty-five cents
See my hound dog bite a rabbit
And my football's sittin' on a barbed-wire fence

Well, my temperature rises and my feet don't walk so fast
Yes, my temperature rises and my feet don't walk so fast
Well, this Arabian doctor came in, gave me a shot
But wouldn't tell me if what I had would last

Well, this woman I've got, she's filling me with her drive
Yes, this woman I've got, she's thrillin' me with her hive
She's calling me Stan
Or else she calls me Mister Clive

Of course, you're gonna think this song is a riff
I know you're gonna think this song is a cliff

坐在带刺铁篱上

我花了一千五百万十二块
　七毛二
我花了一千两百二十七块
　五毛五
看我的猎犬咬兔子
而我的足球坐在带刺铁篱上

哦,我体温上来了所以脚步不那么快
是啊,我体温上来了所以脚步不那么快
哦,阿拉伯医生来了,给了我一针
却不肯告诉我这病是否还会持续

哦,我有个女人,用她的动力给我加满
是啊,我有个女人,用她的蜂房给我震撼
她现在叫我斯坦
但平时叫我克莱夫先生

当然啦,你会认为这歌就是个反复段 [1]
我知道你会觉得这歌很惊险

---

[1] 反复段(riff),爵士乐和摇滚乐中即兴反复演奏的乐句,以不断反复制造兴奋情绪。

Unless you've been inside a tunnel
And fell down 69, 70 feet over a barbed-wire fence

All night!

除非你已经进了隧道
从 69、70 英尺的带刺铁篱上摔下来

通宵达旦!

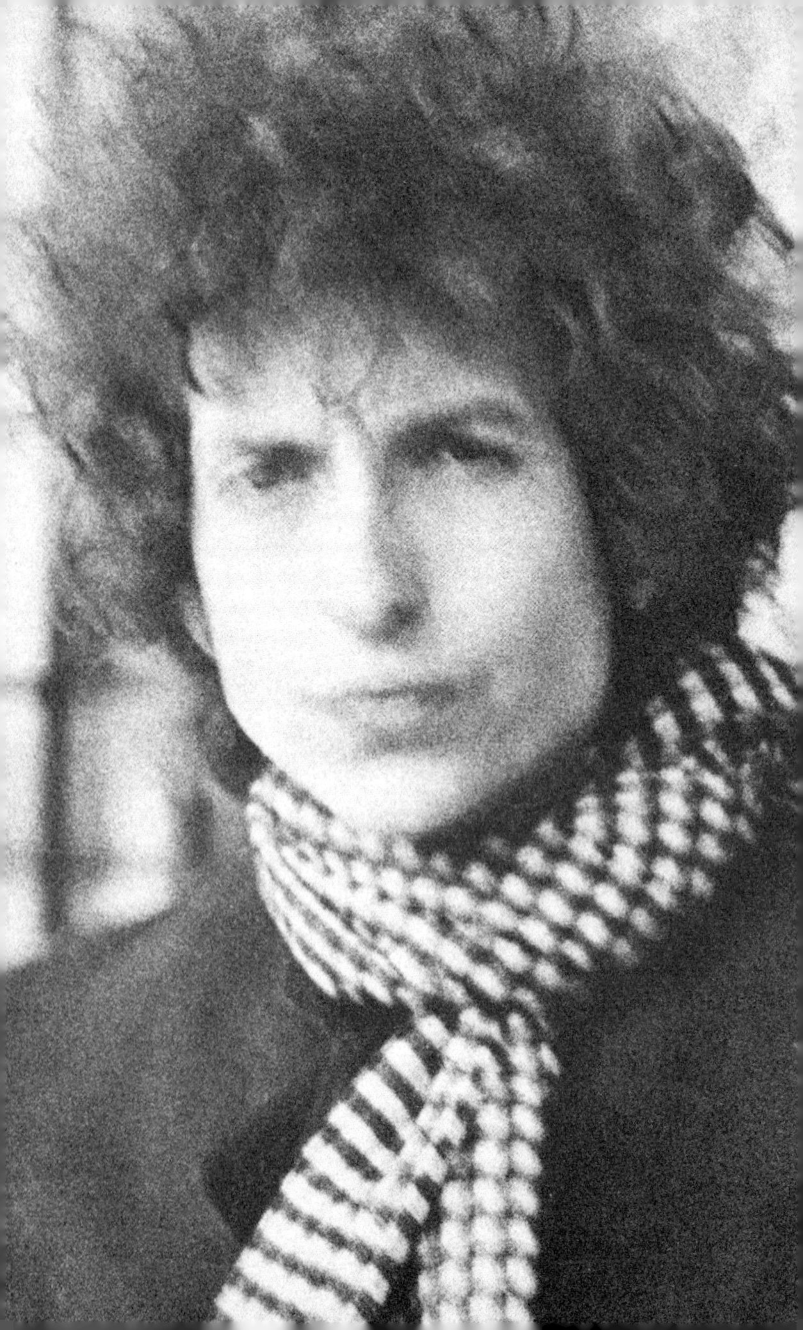

BLONDE ON BLONDE
金发叠金发

雨天女人 12 与 35 号

抵押我的时间

乔安娜的幻影

我们总有一个人要明白(迟早的事)

我要你

再次困在莫比尔和孟菲斯蓝调一起

豹皮药盒帽

就像个女人

多半是你走你的道(而我过我的桥)

像阿喀琉斯一样短命

绝对的甜蜜玛丽

第四次左右

分明五位信徒

低地的愁容夫人

附加歌词

我会把它当自己的事 告诉我,妈妈
我要做你情人 她现在是你的人了

2. i got 14 fevers/ i got 5 believers...dressed up like men
   tell your mama not to worry/

2. (a) tell your mama & your pappa i'm trying to keep from dying to

3. tell your mama & your pappa that there's nothing wrong with my
   jugler vein
   tell your mama i love her & tell your sister Alice the same
   Lonely Lonely miss.

4. (comes from) (ing)
   when you sleep on windows & you stay up all nite swallowing rocks
   making love to / making love to

5. i shoulda sent her to Hong Kong stead of leaving

迪伦这第 7 张录音室专辑，专辑名究竟是什么意思？我们就不纠结了，它在摇滚乐历史上真正是笔糊涂账。从字面理解，辅以中文的组词造句法，《金发叠金发》或许是最优解。

2016 年，鲍勃·迪伦获得诺贝尔文学奖。当有人问起如何评价迪伦的文学价值时，瑞典文学院秘书萨拉·达尼乌斯（Sara Danius）说，建议先听听《金发叠金发》。

《金发叠金发》由哥伦比亚唱片公司于 1966 年 5 月 16 日发行。自《全部带回家》于 1965 年 3 月 22 日出版算起，在不到 15 个月的时间里，迪伦连续推出了 3 张惊世大作，一张比一张生猛，一张比一张分量更重。《金发叠金发》长达 72 分 57 秒，包含 14 首歌曲、2 张唱片，将迪伦此前开启的民谣融合摇滚、摇滚融合现代主义诗歌的风格，引向了一个新高度。迪伦的"摇滚三部曲"从半电声到全电声，从概念专辑到双唱片概念专辑，使流行音乐自此具有了容量巨大的形式，一张专辑丝毫不亚于一本诗集，并且，令人难以想象的是，它面向的是当代大众。

专辑于 1965 年 10 月 5 日在纽约开始录音。从民谣突围而出的迪伦此时备受舆论压力，处于更具有创造力却也是一片混沌的状态。他与加拿大"乐队"（the Band）的传奇合作，即从此时开始。这场合作以一地鸡毛开场，在断断续续4个月的时间里，只成功完成了1首收入专辑的歌曲。

阴差阳错，也可以说是因缘际会，在制作人约翰斯顿的建议下，录音移师"乡村音乐之都"纳什维尔。1966年2月14至17日和3月8至10日，迪伦与纳什维尔的"棚虫"及身边乐手，半即兴地录制完成了专辑中另外13首歌曲。

这张专辑展示了摇滚乐历史上最惊人的语言和声音爆发，也带来了新的歌曲创作方式。在一种半预期的情形下（事先，阿尔·库珀会将迪伦已有的歌曲动机试奏给乐手们），迪伦与乐手们一起行动，即兴合奏录音。有评论说，这张专辑是纳什维尔音乐家的专业知识与现代主义文学敏感性的联姻；也有人说它的歌词是幻想与口语的独特结合，充满了既出世又放荡的天才气息。

《雨天女人12与35号》在一支由疯子组成的救世军乐队的进行曲中开场。迪伦此时以更明白自己处境的、更优越的姿态创作，重点已不在对被人迫害的愤怒，而在轻飘飘的波希米亚式醉态。《抵押我的时间》以变形的布鲁斯，继续这场晕晕乎乎的玩世闹剧。《乔安娜的幻影》将模糊的时间与意识、幻觉与妄想奇妙地现实化了……成功地以生动、即时的方式写下了最初始的感情。

《再次困在莫比尔和孟菲斯蓝调一起》将城市布鲁斯的强力循环、旋涡般的电声音流结构，与荒诞的现代叙事成功结合，表现了现代人"鬼撞墙"的困境。《我要你》

《豹皮药盒帽》《绝对的甜蜜玛丽》《分明五位信徒》《第四次左右》都成功地将这种城市布鲁斯与现代文学进行了奇妙结合，展示了迪伦处理主题的轻巧、语言表现力的直接和令人喷饭的讽刺。它们以传统的再生，以通俗与前卫的连接，以黑人文化的性隐喻，以底层的语言直白但话里有话的表达方式，将布鲁斯文学端上了现代主义的台面。

《就像个女人》与《低地的愁容夫人》两首刻画女性形象的杰作，也都运用民歌手法，将抒情和评论交付叙事，达到了一次表达、以一抵三的效果。《就像个女人》一唱三叹，似无情批判又似至高赞美，简洁而又隽永绵长。《低地的愁容夫人》是迪伦为第一任妻子萨拉·朗兹（Sara Lownds）创作的"婚礼歌曲"。歌词充满古典气息，词汇和意象又是现代的，难以想象这幅为妻子绘制的画像，孤苦而隐忍，有着神圣和黑暗的双重属性，但是她的美以及力量，因此显得神秘、内在、悠远而强大。专辑中几乎处处都在显示迪伦的这种能力：将复杂的思想和不羁的哲学融入简短诗句和令人惊叹的意象中。

通过这张专辑，迪伦终于施展创造力，录制出了他想要的理想声音。1978年，迪伦这样描述："它是一种纤薄、狂野的水银样的声音，有着金属色和亮金色，连带着它召唤出来的一切。"

RAINY DAY WOMEN #12 & 35

Well, they'll stone ya when you're trying to be so good
They'll stone ya just a-like they said they would
They'll stone ya when you're tryin' to go home
Then they'll stone ya when you're there all alone
But I would not feel so all alone
Everybody must get stoned

Well, they'll stone ya when you're walkin' 'long the street
They'll stone ya when you're tryin' to keep your seat
They'll stone ya when you're walkin' on the floor
They'll stone ya when you're walkin' to the door
But I would not feel so all alone
Everybody must get stoned

They'll stone ya when you're at the breakfast table
They'll stone ya when you are young and able
They'll stone ya when you're tryin' to make a buck
They'll stone ya and then they'll say, "good luck"
Tell ya what, I would not feel so all alone
Everybody must get stoned

Well, they'll stone you and say that it's the end

雨天女人 12 与 35 号

哦,他们朝你扔石头当你正努力做好人
他们朝你扔石头就像他们说好了要这么干
他们朝你扔石头当你正努力往家赶
然后他们就朝你扔石头当你孤孤单单
可我不觉得有多孤单
人人都得被扔石头

哦,他们朝你扔石头当你正走在街上
他们朝你扔石头当你想留个位子
他们朝你扔石头当你在屋里踱来踱去
他们朝你扔石头当你踱到了门口
可我不觉得有多孤单
人人都得被扔石头

他们朝你扔石头当你正吃着早餐
他们朝你扔石头当你年轻正能干
他们朝你扔石头当你在努力挣钱
他们朝你扔石头然后喊:"祝你好运"
告诉你吧,我不觉得有多孤单
人人都得被扔石头

哦,他们朝你扔石头说这就是结局

Then they'll stone you and then they'll come back again
They'll stone you when you're riding in your car
They'll stone you when you're playing your guitar
Yes, but I would not feel so all alone
Everybody must get stoned

Well, they'll stone you when you walk all alone
They'll stone you when you are walking home
They'll stone you and then say you are brave
They'll stone you when you are set down in your grave
But I would not feel so all alone
Everybody must get stoned

然后他们朝你扔石头然后回头再扔一次
他们朝你扔石头当你正开着车
他们朝你扔石头当你正弹着吉他
是的,可我不觉得有多孤单
人人都得被扔石头

哦,他们朝你扔石头当你独自上路
他们朝你扔石头当你踏上归途
他们朝你扔石头然后说你很勇敢
他们朝你扔石头当你被放入坟墓
可我不觉得有多孤单
人人都得被扔石头

PLEDGING MY TIME

Well, early in the mornin'
'Til late at night
I got a poison headache
But I feel all right
I'm pledging my time to you
Hopin' you'll come through, too

Well, the hobo jumped up
He came down natur'lly
After he stole my baby
Then he wanted to steal me
But I'm pledging my time to you
Hopin' you'll come through, too

Won't you come with me, baby?
I'll take you where you wanna go
And if it don't work out
You'll be the first to know
I'm pledging my time to you
Hopin' you'll come through, too

Well, the room is so stuffy

抵押我的时间

唉,从一大早
一直到深夜
头疼得像中了毒
可我感觉挺不错
我把时间抵押给你
希望你也能挺过去

唉,那流浪汉跳起来
又自然地落下去
偷走了我的宝贝儿
还想把我也偷走
不过我把时间抵押给你
希望你也能挺过去

你不跟我来吗,宝贝儿?
想去哪儿,我带你去
万一实在没法搞
你也可以第一个知道
我把时间抵押给你
希望你也能挺过去

唉,房间里太挤

I can hardly breathe
Ev'rybody's gone but me and you
And I can't be the last to leave
I'm pledging my time to you
Hopin' you'll come through, too

Well, they sent for the ambulance
And one was sent
Somebody got lucky
But it was an accident
Now I'm pledging my time to you
Hopin' you'll come through, too

我简直没法呼吸
所有人都走了,只剩我和你
而我不能最后撤离
我把时间抵押给你
希望你也能挺过去

唉,他们叫来了救护车
一个人被抬了上去
这人走运啊
只不过是场意外
既然我把时间抵押给你
就希望你也能挺过去

VISIONS OF JOHANNA

Ain't it just like the night to play tricks when you're trying to be so quiet?
We sit here stranded, though we're all doin' our best to deny it
And Louise holds a handful of rain, temptin' you to defy it
Lights flicker from the opposite loft
In this room the heat pipes just cough
The country music station plays soft
But there's nothing, really nothing to turn off
Just Louise and her lover so entwined
And these visions of Johanna that conquer my mind

In the empty lot where the ladies play blindman's bluff with the key chain
And the all-night girls they whisper of escapades out on the "D" train
We can hear the night watchman click his flashlight
Ask himself if it's him or them that's really insane
Louise, she's all right, she's just near
She's delicate and seems like the mirror
But she just makes it all too concise and too clear

乔安娜的幻影 [1]

不就是那种作弄人的夜晚,而你尽力想保持
　一份宁静?
我们被困坐在这里,尽管每人都极力否认
而路易丝捧来了一捧雨水,诱引你无视这一切
对面阁楼灯火闪闪烁烁
这个房间的暖气管只是咳嗽
乡村电台音乐轻柔
但没有什么,真没有什么是要关掉的
只是路易丝和她的情人在这般缠绵
而乔安娜的种种幻影,占据了我的心

空地上,女士们用钥匙链在玩
　捉迷藏
而通宵女郎,低声说着地铁 D 线上的
　恶作剧
我们能听见守夜人在开关手电筒
他问自己到底是他还是他们,真的疯了
路易丝,她浑然无事,就在近旁
纤弱娇美像一面镜子
却也让一切太过明明白白清清楚楚

---

[1] 本篇由杨盈盈校译。

That Johanna's not here
The ghost of 'lectricity howls in the bones of her face
Where these visions of Johanna have now taken my place

Now, little boy lost, he takes himself so seriously
He brags of his misery, he likes to live dangerously
And when bringing her name up
He speaks of a farewell kiss to me
He's sure got a lotta gall to be so useless and all
Muttering small talk at the wall while I'm in the hall
How can I explain?
Oh, it's so hard to get on
And these visions of Johanna, they kept me up past the dawn

Inside the museums, Infinity goes up on trial
Voices echo this is what salvation must be like after a while
But Mona Lisa musta had the highway blues
You can tell by the way she smiles
See the primitive wallflower freeze
When the jelly-faced women all sneeze
Hear the one with the mustache say, "Jeeze
I can't find my knees"
Oh, jewels and binoculars hang from the head of the mule
But these visions of Johanna, they make it all seem so cruel

乔安娜不在这儿

电气幽灵在她的脸骨中嚎叫

那里,乔安娜的种种幻影,取代了我的位置

如今,小男孩迷了路,他太拿自己当回事

他吹嘘自己的不幸,他喜欢过危险的生活

可当提及她的名字

他对我说起一个告别之吻

他定有许多苦衷,才变得这么没用

对着墙壁叽叽咕咕,当我人在大厅里

我该怎么解释?

啊,这实在难说下去

于是乔安娜的种种幻影,让我彻夜不眠直到天色微明

博物馆里,"永恒"升起受到审判

众声回响:不久后救赎一定就是这般情形

但是蒙娜丽莎想必怀有那公路蓝调

从她微笑的样子,你应该能读懂

看到古代的壁花[1]就这样被封存

当果冻脸的女人们喷嚏连声

就听留小胡子的那位说:"天哪

我找不到我的膝盖了"

啊,珠宝和双筒望远镜挂在骡子头上

但是乔安娜的种种幻影,让这一切看起来如此无情

---

[1] 壁花,在社交场合因害羞而没有舞伴或不与人交谈的人。

The peddler now speaks to the countess who's pretending to care for him

Sayin', "Name me someone that's not a parasite and I'll go out and say a prayer for him"

But like Louise always says

"Ya can't look at much, can ya man?"

As she, herself, prepares for him

And Madonna, she still has not showed

We see this empty cage now corrode

Where her cape of the stage once had flowed

The fiddler, he now steps to the road

He writes ev'rything's been returned which was owed

On the back of the fish truck that loads

While my conscience explodes

The harmonicas play the skeleton keys and the rain

And these visions of Johanna are now all that remain

现在小贩对假意关心他的伯爵夫人
   开口道
"告诉我谁不是寄生虫,我出去为他
   祈祷"
但就像路易丝常说的
"你看不了太多,是吧老弟?"
当她,她自己,为他做了准备
圣母玛利亚,依然没露面
我们眼见这空空的囚笼,如今已朽坏
她登台的披肩,一度在那儿垂摆
提琴手,现在踏上了路途
他写道:所有亏欠的,悉数奉还
在满载的贩鱼车后面
我的良心怦然爆炸
口琴们奏起万能曲调[1]和雨水
而乔安娜的种种幻影,是现在仅存的唯一东西

---

[1] 万能曲调,同时有"万能钥匙"之意,字面意思是"骷髅钥匙、骷髅曲调"。

ONE OF US MUST KNOW
(SOONER OR LATER)

I didn't mean to treat you so bad
You shouldn't take it so personal
I didn't mean to make you so sad
You just happened to be there, that's all
When I saw you say "goodbye" to your friend and smile
I thought that it was well understood
That you'd be comin' back in a little while
I didn't know that you were sayin' "goodbye" for good

But, sooner or later, one of us must know
You just did what you're supposed to do
Sooner or later, one of us must know
That I really did try to get close to you

I couldn't see what you could show me
Your scarf had kept your mouth well hid
I couldn't see how you could know me
But you said you knew me and I believed you did
When you whispered in my ear
And asked me if I was leavin' with you or her
I didn't realize just what I did hear

我们总有一个人要明白
（迟早的事）

不是我存心对你坏
你不要以为那是针对个人
不是我存心教你难过
你只是碰巧在那，仅此而已
见你微笑着和朋友说"再见"
我想事情已经很清楚
你过会儿就会回来
却未料到你说的"再见"是永别

不过，迟早的事，我们总有一个人要明白
你只是做了你应该做的
迟早的事，我们总有一个人要明白
我真的努力过，想要贴近你

我看不出你能给我看什么
围巾把你的嘴遮得严严实实
我看不出你怎么可能了解我
但你说你了解，我也就信了
当你在我耳边低语
问我是跟你走还是跟她走
我没明白我到底听到了什么

I didn't realize how young you were

But, sooner or later, one of us must know
You just did what you're supposed to do
Sooner or later, one of us must know
That I really did try to get close to you

I couldn't see when it started snowin'
Your voice was all that I heard
I couldn't see where we were goin'
But you said you knew an' I took your word
And then you told me later, as I apologized
That you were just kiddin' me, you weren't really from the farm
An' I told you, as you clawed out my eyes
That I never really meant to do you any harm

But, sooner or later, one of us must know
You just did what you're supposed to do
Sooner or later, one of us must know
That I really did try to get close to you

我没明白你有多年幼

不过，迟早的事，我们总有一个人要明白
你只是做了你应该做的
迟早的事，我们总有一个人要明白
我真的努力过，想要贴近你

我没发觉雪什么时候开始下
我听见的全是你的声音
我没瞧见我们要去哪里
但你说你知道，我相信了你的话
后来我道了歉，你才告诉我
之前你只是开玩笑，你并非来自农场
而我告诉你，你挖我眼睛时
我真的从没想过要伤害你

不过，迟早的事，我们总有一个人要明白
你只是做了你应该做的
迟早的事，我们总有一个人要明白
我真的努力过，想要贴近你

I WANT YOU

The guilty undertaker sighs
The lonesome organ grinder cries
The silver saxophones say I should refuse you
The cracked bells and washed-out horns
Blow into my face with scorn
But it's not that way
I wasn't born to lose you

I want you, I want you
I want you so bad
Honey, I want you

The drunken politician leaps
Upon the street where mothers weep
And the saviors who are fast asleep, they wait for you
And I wait for them to interrupt
Me drinkin' from my broken cup
And ask me to
Open up the gate for you

I want you, I want you
I want you so bad

我要你

那负疚的入殓师叹息
那寂寞的手摇风琴手哭泣
那银色萨克斯管说我该拒绝你
那裂开的铃和褪色的号
将嘲笑吹到我脸上
但是不该这样
我不是命中注定要失去你

我要你,我要你
我多么想要你
亲爱的,我要你

那醉酒的政客大步跳跃
穿过母亲们啜泣的街
快速入睡的救星们,他们在等你
而我在等他们叫停
叫我不再用破杯狂饮
叫我去为你
打开大门

我要你,我要你
我多么想要你

Honey, I want you

How all my fathers, they've gone down
True love they've been without it
But all their daughters put me down
'Cause I don't think about it

Well, I return to the Queen of Spades
And talk with my chambermaid
She knows that I'm not afraid to look at her
She is good to me
And there's nothing she doesn't see
She knows where I'd like to be
But it doesn't matter

I want you, I want you
I want you so bad
Honey, I want you

Now your dancing child with his Chinese suit
He spoke to me, I took his flute
No, I wasn't very cute to him, was I?
But I did it, though, because he lied
Because he took you for a ride
And because time was on his side
And because I . . .

亲爱的，我要你

我的所有父辈，他们如何过来
却没有真正的爱
可他们所有的女儿，全都奚落我
因为我对此不以为意

好了，我回到黑桃皇后那里
和女招待说话
她知道我不怕看她
她对我好
而没什么事瞒得了她
她知道我想去哪儿
不过这都无所谓

我要你，我要你
我多么想要你
亲爱的，我要你

眼下你的跳舞小孩，一身中式套装
他与我交谈，我拿走了他的笛子
是的，我不是很招他喜欢，是吧？
可我这么做，只是，因为他撒谎
因为他拿你消遣
还因为时间在他那边
还因为我……

I want you, I want you
I want you so bad
Honey, I want you

我要你,我要你
我多么想要你
亲爱的,我要你

STUCK INSIDE OF MOBILE WITH THE MEMPHIS BLUES AGAIN

Oh, the ragman draws circles
Up and down the block
I'd ask him what the matter was
But I know that he don't talk
And the ladies treat me kindly
And furnish me with tape
But deep inside my heart
I know I can't escape
Oh, Mama, can this really be the end
To be stuck inside of Mobile
With the Memphis blues again

Well, Shakespeare, he's in the alley
With his pointed shoes and his bells
Speaking to some French girl
Who says she knows me well
And I would send a message

再次困在莫比尔和孟菲斯蓝调一起 [1]

啊,那收破烂的画着圈
走来走去在同一个街区打转
我想问他这到底怎么回事
可我知道他缄口不言
女士们都待我很好
给我提供布条
但是我心里明白
不可能逃得出去
唉,妈妈,这事可否就到此为止
再次困在莫比尔
和孟菲斯蓝调一起

哦,莎士比亚在小巷里
穿着尖头鞋,戴着铃铛
和一个法国姑娘在说话
而她说跟我是老相识
我本想捎个信儿

---

[1] 莫比尔,地名,位于美国亚拉巴马州。孟菲斯蓝调,"蓝调之父" W. C. 汉迪有同名歌曲,是"蓝调"一词在书面上的最早记载。本篇由杨盈盈校译。

To find out if she's talked
But the post office has been stolen
And the mailbox is locked
Oh, Mama, can this really be the end
To be stuck inside of Mobile
With the Memphis blues again

Mona tried to tell me
To stay away from the train line
She said that all the railroad men
Just drink up your blood like wine
An' I said, "Oh, I didn't know that
But then again, there's only one I've met
An' he just smoked my eyelids
An' punched my cigarette"
Oh, Mama, can this really be the end
To be stuck inside of Mobile
With the Memphis blues again

Grandpa died last week
And now he's buried in the rocks
But everybody still talks about
How badly they were shocked
But me, I expected it to happen
I knew he'd lost control
When he built a fire on Main Street

看她是否真这么说了
但是邮局被盗
信箱也上了锁
唉,妈妈,这事可否就到此为止
再次困在莫比尔
和孟菲斯蓝调一起

莫娜极力劝诫我
要离铁路线远点儿
她说那些铁路工
都会像喝酒一样把你的血喝干了
我说:"哦,不知道还有这等事
但话说回来,我碰到过一回
但他只是朝我的眼皮喷烟
还挥拳揍了我的烟卷"
唉,妈妈,这事可否就到此为止
再次困在莫比尔
和孟菲斯蓝调一起

爷爷上星期去世了
现在葬在岩石堆里
但大家都还在议论
说他们是多么震惊
但是我,早有预感
我知道他老早就疯了
竟在大街上生火

And shot it full of holes
Oh, Mama, can this really be the end
To be stuck inside of Mobile
With the Memphis blues again

Now the senator came down here
Showing ev'ryone his gun
Handing out free tickets
To the wedding of his son
An' me, I nearly got busted
An' wouldn't it be my luck
To get caught without a ticket
And be discovered beneath a truck
Oh, Mama, can this really be the end
To be stuck inside of Mobile
With the Memphis blues again

Now the preacher looked so baffled
When I asked him why he dressed
With twenty pounds of headlines
Stapled to his chest
But he cursed me when I proved it to him
Then I whispered, "Not even you can hide
You see, you're just like me
I hope you're satisfied"
Oh, Mama, can this really be the end

还开枪轰得它满是洞
唉,妈妈,这事可否就到此为止
再次困在莫比尔
和孟菲斯蓝调一起

你看,参议员也来了
给每个人秀他的枪
还到处发赠票
叫人参加他儿子的婚礼
我呢,差一点儿被捕
实在是运气差
因为没有票
被人从卡车底下揪了出来
唉,妈妈,这事可否就到此为止
再次困在莫比尔
和孟菲斯蓝调一起

瞧,牧师看来大惑不解
我问他为什么这样打扮
要把二十磅重的新闻标题
钉在胸口
我指给他看,却引得他破口大骂
我只好小声说:"连你也藏不住
你看,你就跟我一样
祝你称心如意"
唉,妈妈,这事可否就到此为止

To be stuck inside of Mobile
With the Memphis blues again

Now the rainman gave me two cures
Then he said, "Jump right in"
The one was Texas medicine
The other was just railroad gin
An' like a fool I mixed them
An' it strangled up my mind
An' now people just get uglier
An' I have no sense of time
Oh, Mama, can this really be the end
To be stuck inside of Mobile
With the Memphis blues again

When Ruthie says come see her
In her honky-tonk lagoon
Where I can watch her waltz for free
'Neath her Panamanian moon
An' I say, "Aw come on now
You must know about my debutante"
An' she says, "Your debutante just knows what you need

再次困在莫比尔

和孟菲斯蓝调一起

这会儿,雨人给了我两服药

然后说:"马上服下"

一服是得州良药 [1]

一服是铁路杜松子酒

像个傻瓜,我将两者混起来

结果它扼住了我的大脑

使人人看上去更加丑陋

我的时间概念也没了

唉,妈妈,这事可否就到此为止

再次困在莫比尔

和孟菲斯蓝调一起

露丝叫我去看她

她在小酒馆咸水池

我可以免费看她跳华尔兹

在她的巴拿马月光里

我说:"少来啦

你应该知道我家元媛 [2]"

她说:"你家元媛只知道你需要什么

---

[1] 得州良药,致幻剂麦司卡林的俗称,以美墨边境生长的仙人掌提炼而成。
[2] 元媛(debutante),初进社交界的上流社会年轻女子。

But I know what you want"
Oh, Mama, can this really be the end
To be stuck inside of Mobile
With the Memphis blues again

Now the bricks lay on Grand Street
Where the neon madmen climb
They all fall there so perfectly
It all seems so well timed
An' here I sit so patiently
Waiting to find out what price
You have to pay to get out of
Going through all these things twice
Oh, Mama, can this really be the end
To be stuck inside of Mobile
With the Memphis blues again

我却知道什么是你向往的"
唉,妈妈,这事可否就到此为止
再次困在莫比尔
和孟菲斯蓝调一起

这会儿,砖头堆在格兰大街
霓虹灯疯子都在往上爬
砖头完美地掉下来
像是时间经过了精确设计
而我耐心地坐在这儿
等着搞明白
须付出怎样的代价
才可避免让这些事重来一遍
唉,妈妈,这事可否就到此为止
再次困在莫比尔
和孟菲斯蓝调一起

LEOPARD-SKIN PILL-BOX HAT

Well, I see you got your brand new leopard-skin pill-box hat
Yes, I see you got your brand new leopard-skin pill-box hat
Well, you must tell me, baby
How your head feels under somethin' like that
Under your brand new leopard-skin pill-box hat

Well, you look so pretty in it
Honey, can I jump on it sometime?
Yes, I just wanna see
If it's really that expensive kind
You know it balances on your head
Just like a mattress balances
On a bottle of wine
Your brand new leopard-skin pill-box hat

Well, if you wanna see the sun rise
Honey, I know where
We'll go out and see it sometime
We'll both just sit there and stare

豹皮药盒帽 [1]

好呀,我看你有了崭新的豹皮药盒帽
是呀,我看你有了崭新的豹皮药盒帽
好呀,你一定要告诉我,阿宝
你的脑袋在那玩意儿下是什么感觉
你崭新的豹皮药盒帽

好呀,你戴上它真漂亮极了
亲爱的,我能找个时间跳上去吗?
是呀,我只是想看看
它到底是不是很名贵的那款
知道吧,它在你头上保持着平衡
就像一张床垫
在一瓶酒上保持着平衡
你崭新的豹皮药盒帽

好呀,如果你想看日出
亲爱的,我知道地点
我们找个时间看日出吧
我们俩就坐那儿盯着看

---

[1] 当时流行的一种帽子,肯尼迪总统发表就职演说时,他的夫人杰奎琳就戴着这款帽子。

Me with my belt
Wrapped around my head
And you just sittin' there
In your brand new leopard-skin pill-box hat

Well, I asked the doctor if I could see you
It's bad for your health, he said
Yes, I disobeyed his orders
I came to see you
But I found him there instead
You know, I don't mind him cheatin' on me
But I sure wish he'd take that off his head
Your brand new leopard-skin pill-box hat

Well, I see you got a new boyfriend
You know, I never seen him before
Well, I saw him
Makin' love to you
You forgot to close the garage door
You might think he loves you for your money
But I know what he really loves you for
It's your brand new leopard-skin pill-box hat

我用我的皮带
箍着脑袋
你呢也坐在那儿
戴着你崭新的豹皮药盒帽

好呀，我问医生能不能去看你
他说，这对你健康不利
是呀，我违背了他的指令
跑去看你
却发现他却在你这里
你知道，我不介意他跟我耍阴招儿
可我真想他把那玩意儿从头上摘掉
你崭新的豹皮药盒帽

好呀，我看见你有了新男友
知道吧，我以前从没见过他
好呀，我看见他了
在和你做爱
你们忘记关车库门了
你可能以为他爱你是图你的钱
但我知道他爱你真正的原因
是你崭新的豹皮药盒帽

JUST LIKE A WOMAN

Nobody feels any pain
Tonight as I stand inside the rain
Ev'rybody knows
That Baby's got new clothes
But lately I see her ribbons and her bows
Have fallen from her curls
She takes just like a woman, yes, she does
She makes love just like a woman, yes, she does
And she aches just like a woman
But she breaks just like a little girl

Queen Mary, she's my friend
Yes, I believe I'll go see her again
Nobody has to guess
That Baby can't be blessed
Till she sees finally that she's like all the rest
With her fog, her amphetamine and her pearls
She takes just like a woman, yes, she does
She makes love just like a woman, yes, she does

就像个女人 [1]

没有人觉得痛苦
在今晚,当我伫立雨中
每个人都知道
那女孩儿有了新衣裳
但是最近我看见,她的丝带和发卡
已从她的卷发上落下
她拿走东西就像个女人,是的,她拿了
她与人做爱就像个女人,是的,她做了
她感到疼,就像个女人
但是她伤心了,就像一个小姑娘

玛丽女皇,是我的朋友
是的,我相信还会再去看她
人们不用猜就知道
女孩儿会被上帝赐福
她最后会发现,自己原来跟别人一样
陪伴她的是迷雾、安非他明 [2] 和她的珍珠
她拿走东西就像个女人,是的,她拿了
她与人做爱就像个女人,是的,她做了

---

[1] 本篇由郝佳校译。
[2] 安非他明,一种解除忧郁、疲劳的药。

And she aches just like a woman
But she breaks just like a little girl

It was raining from the first
And I was dying there of thirst
So I came in here
And your long-time curse hurts
But what's worse
Is this pain in here
I can't stay in here
Ain't it clear that—

I just can't fit
Yes, I believe it's time for us to quit
When we meet again
Introduced as friends
Please don't let on that you knew me when
I was hungry and it was your world
Ah, you fake just like a woman, yes, you do
You make love just like a woman, yes, you do
Then you ache just like a woman
But you break just like a little girl

她感到疼，就像个女人
但是她伤心了，就像一个小姑娘

从一开始就在下雨
我在那儿却干渴得要死
所以我来到这里
而你长久的诅咒，让人难过
但更坏的是
这儿的痛苦
我不能待在这儿
还不清楚吗……

我真的不能够适应
是的我确信，分手的时候到了
当有一天我们再次相遇
被别人介绍成为朋友
请不要透露你认识我
在我饥渴时，那时是你的世界
啊，你骗人的样子就像个女人，是的，你骗了
你与人做爱就像个女人，是的，你做了
然后你感到疼，就像个女人
但是你伤心了，就像一个小姑娘

MOST LIKELY YOU GO YOUR WAY
(AND I'LL GO MINE)

You say you love me

And you're thinkin' of me

But you know you could be wrong

You say you told me

That you wanna hold me

But you know you're not that strong

I just can't do what I done before

I just can't beg you anymore

I'm gonna let you pass

And I'll go last

Then time will tell just who fell

And who's been left behind

When you go your way and I go mine

You say you disturb me

And you don't deserve me

But you know sometimes you lie

You say you're shakin'

And you're always achin'

But you know how hard you try

Sometimes it gets so hard to care

多半是你走你的道
（而我过我的桥）

你说你爱我
并且你在想我
可是你知道你可能会弄错
你说你对我说过
你想抱着我
可是你知道你不是那么有力气
我做不到以前的事了
我没有办法再向你求乞
我让你先走
我走在最后
时间将证明谁会跌倒
又是谁被抛在了后面
就让你走你的道而我过我的桥

你说你打扰我了
并且你配不上我
可是你知道有时候你真会瞎说
你说你在颤抖
并且你总是很疼
可是你知道你有多努力
有时候真是很难去在乎

It can't be this way ev'rywhere
And I'm gonna let you pass
Yes, and I'll go last
Then time will tell just who fell
And who's been left behind
When you go your way and I go mine

The judge, he holds a grudge
He's gonna call on you
But he's badly built
And he walks on stilts
Watch out he don't fall on you

You say you're sorry
For tellin' stories
That you know I believe are true
You say ya got some
Other kinda lover
And yes, I believe you do
You say my kisses are not like his
But this time I'm not gonna tell you why that is
I'm just gonna let you pass
Yes, and I'll go last
Then time will tell who fell
And who's been left behind
When you go your way and I go mine

但事情总不能永远就这样
所以我让你先走
是的,我走在最后
时间将证明谁会跌倒
又是谁被抛在了后面
就让你走你的道而我过我的桥

那法官他记仇了
他会去找你
但他的体格糟糕
所以他一路踩着高跷
小心别让他砸到你

你说你很抱歉
之前编造了故事
你知道我会深信不疑
你说你找到了
一位不一样的情人
很好,我相信你
你说我的吻不像他
但这次我不会告诉你原因
我只是让你先走
是的,我走在最后
时间将证明谁会跌倒
又是谁被抛在了后面
就让你走你的道而我过我的桥

TEMPORARY LIKE ACHILLES

Standing on your window, honey
Yes, I've been here before
Feeling so harmless
I'm looking at your second door
How come you don't send me no regards?
You know I want your lovin'
Honey, why are you so hard?

Kneeling 'neath your ceiling
Yes, I guess I'll be here for a while
I'm tryin' to read your portrait, but
I'm helpless, like a rich man's child
How come you send someone out to have me barred?
You know I want your lovin'
Honey, why are you so hard?

Like a poor fool in his prime

像阿喀琉斯[1]一样短命

我站在你的窗前,亲爱的
是的,之前我就来过
感觉是这样无足轻重
现在我正望着你内室的门
你怎么能不来问候一声?
明知道我需要你的爱
亲爱的,你为何还要这么冷酷?

跪在你的屋宇下啊
是的,我想我还会待会儿
想读懂你的画像,只是
这么无助,就像一个富家子弟
你怎么能差人出来拦阻?
明知道我需要你的爱
亲爱的,你为何还要这么冷酷?

就像正当年的可怜傻瓜

---

[1] 阿喀琉斯,希腊神话人物,是凡人珀琉斯和仙女忒提斯的儿子。忒提斯为了让儿子成为不死之身,在他出生时将其倒提着浸入冥河。但他被母亲捏住的脚后跟露在水外,成了全身唯一的"死穴"。后来特洛伊战争,太阳神阿波罗射中了他的脚踝,阿喀琉斯死去。

Yes, I know you can hear me walk

But is your heart made out of stone, or is it lime

Or is it just solid rock?

Well, I rush into your hallway

Lean against your velvet door

I watch upon your scorpion

Who crawls across your circus floor

Just what do you think you have to guard?

You know I want your lovin'

Honey, but you're so hard

Achilles is in your alleyway

He don't want me here, he does brag

He's pointing to the sky

And he's hungry, like a man in drag

How come you get someone like him to be your guard?

You know I want your lovin'

Honey, but you're so hard

是的,我知道你听得见我的脚步
可你的心是石头做的吗,或者是石灰
或者就是坚硬的岩石?

好吧,我冲进了你家门厅
靠着你的丝绒门
观察着你的蝎子
从你的马戏场的地上爬过
到底是什么,你一意要保护的?
明知道我需要你的爱
亲爱的,但你就是这么冷酷

阿喀琉斯在你的走廊上
他不让我待这儿,他满嘴的大话
用手指着天空
而且他很饥渴,像穿了女装的男人
你怎么找这样的人做你的护卫?
明知道我需要你的爱
亲爱的,但你就是这么冷酷

ABSOLUTELY SWEET MARIE

Well, your railroad gate, you know I just can't jump it
Sometimes it gets so hard, you see
I'm just sitting here beating on my trumpet
With all these promises you left for me
But where are you tonight, sweet Marie?

Well, I waited for you when I was half sick
Yes, I waited for you when you hated me
Well, I waited for you inside of the frozen traffic
When you knew I had some other place to be
Now, where are you tonight, sweet Marie?

Well, anybody can be just like me, obviously
But then, now again, not too many can be like you, fortunately

Well, six white horses that you did promise
Were fin'lly delivered down to the penitentiary
But to live outside the law, you must be honest
I know you always say that you agree
But where are you tonight, sweet Marie?

绝对的甜蜜玛丽

唉,你的铁路门,你知道我跳不过
有时候事情如此棘手,这你都瞧见了
我只好在这坐下,敲我的小号
带着你留给我的种种承诺
但是今夜你在哪里,甜蜜玛丽?

唉,病恹恹时我等过你
是的,你恨我时我等过你
唉,塞得死死的车流中我等过你
而你知道我必须赶往别处
那么,今夜你在哪里,甜蜜玛丽?

唉,显然人人都可以像我这样
但话又说回来,幸运的是,没几个人能像你

唉,你许诺过的六匹白马
最后送去了监狱
但是要过法外生活,你必须诚实
我记得你总说你认同这种看法
但是今夜你在哪里,甜蜜玛丽?

---

[1] 本篇由杨盈盈校译。

Well, I don't know how it happened
But the riverboat captain, he knows my fate
But ev'rybody else, even yourself
They're just gonna have to wait

Well, I got the fever down in my pockets
The Persian drunkard, he follows me
Yes, I can take him to your house but I can't unlock it
You see, you forgot to leave me with the key
Oh, where are you tonight, sweet Marie?

Now, I been in jail when all my mail showed
That a man can't give his address out to bad company
And now I stand here lookin' at your yellow railroad
In the ruins of your balcony
Wond'ring where you are tonight, sweet Marie

唉，这是怎么回事我也没闹明白
但是江上的船老大，他知道我的命
不过其他所有人，甚至包括你自己
都没有办法只有等待

唉，我在口袋里发起高烧
那个波斯醉鬼，他跟着我
是的，我可以带他来你家但我开不了锁
你瞧，你忘了给我留钥匙
啊，今夜你在哪里，甜蜜玛丽？

哦，在大牢里的时候，我的每封信都在表明
一个人不该把地址透露给狐朋狗友
此时我站在这儿，在你阳台的废墟
看着你黄色的铁路
在想今夜你在哪里，甜蜜玛丽

FOURTH TIME AROUND

When she said

"Don't waste your words, they're just lies"

I cried she was deaf

And she worked on my face until breaking my eyes

Then said, "What else you got left?"

It was then that I got up to leave

But she said, "Don't forget

Everybody must give something back

For something they get"

I stood there and hummed

I tapped on her drum and asked her how come

And she buttoned her boot

And straightened her suit

Then she said, "Don't get cute"

So I forced my hands in my pockets

And felt with my thumbs

And gallantly handed her

My very last piece of gum

She threw me outside

I stood in the dirt where ev'ryone walked

第四次左右

当她说
"少废话,都是骗人的"
我大喊说她聋了
她修理我的脸直到伤了我的眼
说:"你还有什么?"
就是在那一刻,我起身离开
而她说:"别忘了
任何人为了他所得到的
都必须付出代价"

我站在那儿哼歌
敲着她的鼓,问她怎么回事
她扣好了靴子
抻直衣裳
然后说:"别装"
于是我勉强伸手到衣袋里
用拇指去感觉
殷勤地递给她
我最后一块口香糖

她把我赶了出去
我站在每个人都走过的泥土里

And after finding I'd
Forgotten my shirt
I went back and knocked
I waited in the hallway, she went to get it
And I tried to make sense
Out of that picture of you in your wheelchair
That leaned up against . . .

Her Jamaican rum
And when she did come, I asked her for some
She said, "No, dear"
I said, "Your words aren't clear
You'd better spit out your gum"
She screamed till her face got so red
Then she fell on the floor
And I covered her up and then
Thought I'd go look through her drawer

And when I was through
I filled up my shoe
And brought it to you
And you, you took me in
You loved me then
You didn't waste time
And I, I never took much
I never asked for your crutch
Now don't ask for mine

才发现自己
忘了拿衬衣
我回去敲门
在走廊等,她进屋拿
然后我费力地想弄清楚
那张你坐在轮椅上的照片
轮椅斜靠着……

她的牙买加朗姆酒
这时她总算来了,我要她给我点儿
她说:"不行,亲爱的"
我说:"你口齿不清
最好把口香糖吐掉"
她尖叫,脸变得绯红
然后倒在地上
我把她盖好然后
想我应该翻翻她的抽屉

等我翻完了
把鞋子装满了
就带过来给你
而你呢,你带我进来
你就爱我
你没有浪费时间
而我,从不多拿
从没要过你的拐杖
所以也别打我那副的主意

OBVIOUSLY FIVE BELIEVERS

Early in the mornin'
Early in the mornin'
I'm callin' you to
I'm callin' you to
Please come home
Yes, I guess I could make it without you
If I just didn't feel so all alone

Don't let me down
Don't let me down
I won't let you down
I won't let you down
No I won't
You know I can if you can, honey
But, honey, please don't

I got my black dog barkin'
Black dog barkin'
Yes it is now
Yes it is now
Outside my yard
Yes, I could tell you what he means

分明五位信徒

一大清早
一大清早
我打电话
我打电话
求你回家
是啊，我以为没你也能过
如果不是觉得这么孤独

别让我失望
别让我失望
我不会让你失望
我不会让你失望
是的不会的
你知道你可以我便可以，亲爱的
但是亲爱的，求你别这样

我让我那条黑狗叫
黑狗在叫
是的它现在在叫
是的它现在在叫
在我家院子外
是啊，我可以告诉你他的意思

If I just didn't have to try so hard

Your mama's workin'
Your mama's moanin'
She's cryin' you know
She's tryin' you know
You better go now
Well, I'd tell you what she wants
But I just don't know how

Fifteen jugglers
Fifteen jugglers
Five believers
Five believers
All dressed like men
Tell yo' mama not to worry because
They're just my friends

Early in the mornin'
Early in the mornin'
I'm callin' you to
I'm callin' you to
Please come home
Yes, I could make it without you
If I just did not feel so all alone

如果我不必这么费劲

你妈妈在干活
你妈妈在呻吟
她在哭你知道吧
她在尽力你知道吧
你还是赶紧走好了
好吧,我会告诉你她要什么
可是我不知从何说起

十五个耍把戏的
十五个耍把戏的
五位信徒
五位信徒
都穿得人模人样
叫你妈妈别担心,因为
他们只是我的朋友

一大清早
一大清早
我打电话
我打电话
求你回家
是啊,我以为没你也能过
如果不是觉得这么孤独

SAD-EYED LADY OF THE LOWLANDS

With your mercury mouth in the missionary times
And your eyes like smoke and your prayers like rhymes
And your silver cross, and your voice like chimes
Oh, who among them do they think could bury you?
With your pockets well protected at last
And your streetcar visions which you place on the grass
And your flesh like silk, and your face like glass
Who among them do they think could carry you?
Sad-eyed lady of the lowlands
Where the sad-eyed prophet says that no man comes
My warehouse eyes, my Arabian drums
Should I leave them by your gate
Or, sad-eyed lady, should I wait?

With your sheets like metal and your belt like lace
And your deck of cards missing the jack and the ace
And your basement clothes and your hollow face
Who among them can think he could outguess you?
With your silhouette when the sunlight dims

低地的愁容夫人 [1]

你的水银般的嘴,在传教士的年代
你的眼睛如烟似雾,你的祈祷仿佛诗文
你的银质的十字架,你的声音像钟琴
啊,他们以为他们中的谁,能埋葬你?
终于,你的衣袋保护得完好
你街车的幻影停放在草地上
你的肌肤像丝绸,你的脸仿佛玻璃
他们以为他们中的谁,能带走你?
低地的愁容夫人
愁容的先知预言:你没有男人
我仓库般的眼睛,我的阿拉伯鼓
我是不是要将它们留下,留在你的门边
或者,愁容的夫人,我是否应该等待?

你的床单像金属,你的衣带仿佛花边
你的纸牌,遗失了 J 和 A
你地下室的衣服和你空的脸
他们中到底会有谁,以为能看透你?
阳光转暗时留下你的侧影

---

[1] 这首歌写给迪伦的第一任妻子萨拉·朗兹(Sara Lowndes),迪伦将她的姓名织入歌名。本篇由郝佳校译。

Into your eyes where the moonlight swims
And your matchbook songs and your gypsy hymns
Who among them would try to impress you?
Sad-eyed lady of the lowlands
Where the sad-eyed prophet says that no man comes
My warehouse eyes, my Arabian drums
Should I leave them by your gate
Or, sad-eyed lady, should I wait?

The kings of Tyrus with their convict list
Are waiting in line for their geranium kiss
And you wouldn't know it would happen like this
But who among them really wants just to kiss you?
With your childhood flames on your midnight rug
And your Spanish manners and your mother's drugs
And your cowboy mouth and your curfew plugs
Who among them do you think could resist you?
Sad-eyed lady of the lowlands
Where the sad-eyed prophet says that no man comes
My warehouse eyes, my Arabian drums
Should I leave them by your gate
Or, sad-eyed lady, should I wait?

Oh, the farmers and the businessmen, they all did decide

照进你的眼睛那里有月光浮动
啊你的火柴盒上的歌,你的吉卜赛圣咏
他们以为他们中的谁,竟企图给你印象?
低地的愁容夫人
愁容的先知预言——你没有男人
我仓库般的眼睛,我的阿拉伯鼓
我是不是要将它们留下,留在你的门边
或者,愁容的夫人,我是否应该等待?

推罗[1]的王,拿着他们的黑名单
排队等候着,天竺葵的吻
你没有想到,事情会发展得这样
但他们中的谁,真的只是想吻你?
你午夜小垫子上童年的光辉
你西班牙人的举止,你母亲的麻醉药
你牛仔般的嘴、宵禁的塞子
你以为他们中的谁,能抗拒你?
低地的愁容夫人
愁容的先知预言——你没有男人
我仓库般的眼睛,我的阿拉伯鼓
我是不是要将它们留下,留在你的门边
或者,愁容的夫人,我是否应该等待?

啊,农场主和生意人,他们真的打算

---

[1] 推罗,位于黎巴嫩的腓尼基名城。

To show you the dead angels that they used to hide
But why did they pick you to sympathize with their side?
Oh, how could they ever mistake you?
They wished you'd accepted the blame for the farm
But with the sea at your feet and the phony false alarm
And with the child of a hoodlum wrapped up in your arms
How could they ever, ever persuade you?
Sad-eyed lady of the lowlands
Where the sad-eyed prophet says that no man comes
My warehouse eyes, my Arabian drums
Should I leave them by your gate
Or, sad-eyed lady, should I wait?

With your sheet-metal memory of Cannery Row
And your magazine-husband who one day just had to go
And your gentleness now, which you just can't help but show
Who among them do you think would employ you?
Now you stand with your thief, you're on his parole
With your holy medallion which your fingertips fold
And your saintlike face and your ghostlike soul
Oh, who among them do you think could destroy you?
Sad-eyed lady of the lowlands
Where the sad-eyed prophet says that no man comes
My warehouse eyes, my Arabian drums
Should I leave them by your gate
Or, sad-eyed lady, should I wait?

把他们平时藏起来的死天使，拿给你看
但是他们为什么，竟想博得你的同情？
啊，他们怎么会，竟然错看了你？
他们希望你承担农场失败的责任
但是凭着在你脚下的海和昙花一现的人
凭着你紧抱在怀里的强盗的孩子
他们怎么会，可能说服你？
低地的愁容夫人
愁容的先知预言——你没有男人
我仓库般的眼睛，我的阿拉伯鼓
我是不是要将它们留下，留在你的门边
或者，愁容的夫人，我是否应该等待？

你的关于罐头厂街的金属片的记忆
你的有一天不得不走的杂志丈夫
你的温存如今除了展示已毫无办法
你以为他们中的谁，能享用你？
现在你和你的贼并肩站着，仿佛你和他同被假释
带着你的圣章，圣章用你的指尖包着
啊，你圣女般的脸、幽灵般的灵魂
你以为他们中的谁，能毁灭你？
低地的愁容夫人
愁容的先知预言——你没有男人
我仓库般的眼睛，我的阿拉伯鼓
我是不是要将它留下，留在你的门边
或者，愁容的夫人，我是否应该等待？

I'LL KEEP IT WITH MINE

You will search, babe

At any cost

But how long, babe

Can you search for what's not lost?

Everybody will help you

Some people are very kind

But if I can save you any time

Come on, give it to me

I'll keep it with mine

I can't help it

If you might think I'm odd

If I say I'm not loving you for what you are

But for what you're not

Everybody will help you

Discover what you set out to find

But if I can save you any time

Come on, give it to me

I'll keep it with mine

我会把它当自己的事 [1]

你要去寻找,宝贝
不惜代价
但是这要多久,宝贝
寻找你并没丢失的东西?
大家都会帮你
一些人很有善意
但是如果我能帮你省点儿时间
来吧,这事儿交给我
我会把它当自己的事

我忍不住啊
即便你可能把我当怪物
即便我说我爱你不是因为你是什么
而是因为你不是什么
大家都会帮你
找到你着手在找的东西
但是如果我能帮你省点儿时间
来吧,这事儿交给我
我会把它当自己的事

---

[1] 这首以及之后的三首附加歌词,均为郝佳校译。

The train leaves

At half past ten

But it'll be back tomorrow

Same time again

The conductor he's weary

He's still stuck on the line

But if I can save you any time

Come on, give it to me

I'll keep it with mine

火车离开
在十点半
但明天还会回来
在同一时间
售票员疲惫不堪
他仍然困在这条线上
但是如果我能帮你省点儿时间
来吧,这事儿交给我
我会把它当自己的事

I WANNA BE YOUR LOVER

Well, the rainman comes with his magic wand
And the judge says, "Mona can't have no bond"
And the walls collide, Mona cries
And the rainman leaves in the wolfman's disguise

I wanna be your lover, baby, I wanna be your man
I wanna be your lover, baby
I don't wanna be hers, I wanna be yours

Well, the undertaker in his midnight suit
Says to the masked man, "Ain't you cute!"
Well, the mask man he gets up on the shelf
And he says, "You ain't so bad yourself"

I wanna be your lover, baby, I wanna be your man
I wanna be your lover, baby
I don't wanna be hers, I wanna be yours

我要做你情人

哦,雨人带着他的魔杖来了
而法官说:"莫娜不能保释"
墙相撞,莫娜哭了
雨人披着狼人的伪装离去

我要做你情人,宝贝,我要做你男人 [1]
我要做你情人,宝贝
不做她的,要做你的

哦,入殓师穿着午夜礼服
对蒙面人说:"你好帅!"
哦,蒙面人从高阁上起了身
说:"你也不赖"

我要做你情人,宝贝,我要做你男人
我要做你情人,宝贝
不做她的,要做你的

---

[1] 副歌歌词是对披头士乐队《我要做你男人》("I Wanna Be Your Man")的引用。

Well, jumpin' Judy can't go no higher
She had bullets in her eyes, and they fire
Rasputin he's so dignified
He touched the back of her head an' he died

I wanna be your lover, baby, I wanna be your man
I wanna be your lover, baby
I don't wanna be hers, I wanna be yours

Well, Phaedra with her looking glass
Stretchin' out upon the grass
She gets all messed up and she faints—
That's 'cause she's so obvious and you ain't

I wanna be your lover, baby, I wanna be your man
I wanna be your lover, baby
I don't wanna be hers, I wanna be yours

哦,"跳跳朱迪"[1]不可能跳更高了
她的眼里有子弹,它们开着火
拉斯普京[2]仪态如此庄重
他摸到她的后脑勺,然后就死了

我要做你情人,宝贝,我要做你男人
我要做你情人,宝贝
不做她的,要做你的

哦,淮德拉[3]带着明镜
身体舒展地躺在草坪
她把一切都弄乱了套,她晕了——
那是因为她外露,而你不同

我要做你情人,宝贝,我要做你男人
我要做你情人,宝贝
不做她的,要做你的

---

[1] "跳跳朱迪",美国囚歌中的女性形象,一般认为此名含遭受鞭刑而跳起之意。
[2] 拉斯普京(1869—1916),俄国神秘主义者,据传有超能力,沙皇尼古拉二世的宠臣。
[3] 淮德拉,希腊神话中雅典国王忒修斯的后妻,钟情国王前妻之子希波吕托斯,求爱不遂,羞怒诬蔑希波吕托斯强奸了自己。

TELL ME, MOMMA

Ol' black Bascom, don't break no mirrors
Cold black water dog, make no tears
You say you love me with what may be love
Don't you remember makin' baby love?
Got your steam drill built and you're lookin' for some kid
To get it to work for you like your nine-pound hammer did
But I know that you know that I know that you show
Something is tearing up your mind

Tell me, momma
Tell me, momma
Tell me, momma, what is it?
What's wrong with you this time?

Hey, John, come and get me some candy goods

告诉我,妈妈 [1]

老黑巴斯康 [2],别打了镜子
冷黑水犬,千万莫流泪
你说你爱我,说那可能是爱情
你不记得你示过爱了吗宝贝?
造好了蒸汽钻,你去找小伙儿
让它为你干活儿,像是你的九磅锤 [3]
但是我知道你知道我知道你的表情说明
有些事正在撕裂你的心

告诉我,妈妈
告诉我,妈妈
告诉我,妈妈,发生了什么?
这回你是怎么啦?

喂,约翰,来时给我带些甜品

---

[1] 此诗中的妈妈,是俚语中对情人的昵称。
[2] 似指巴斯康·伦斯福德(1882—1973),美国民歌学者,致力于搜集传统民歌,但其非黑人。
[3] 蒸汽钻和九磅锤,指涉 19 世纪美国民间故事:在开凿切萨皮克与俄亥俄铁路的大本德隧道时,黑人钢钻工约翰·亨利与蒸汽钻比赛在岩石上打炮眼,最后亨利虽获胜,但也劳累致死。

Shucks, it sure feels like it's in the woods
Spend some time on your January trips
You got tombstone moose up and your grave-yard whips
If you're anxious to find out when your friendship's gonna end
Come on, baby, I'm your friend!
And I know that you know that I know that you show
Something is tearing up your mind

Tell me, momma
Tell me, momma
Tell me, momma, what is it?
What's wrong with you this time?

Ohh, we bone the editor, can't get read
But his painted sled, instead it's a bed
Yes, I see you on your window ledge
But I can't tell just how far away you are from the edge
And, anyway, you're just gonna make people jump and roar
Watcha wanna go and do that for?
For I know that you know that I know that you know
Something is tearing up your mind

唉，这感觉真像是身陷于密林 [1]
在一月份的旅行上花些时日
你有墓碑驼鹿耸起和你的墓地鞭子 [2]
若你急于知道友情何时到头
来吧宝贝，我是你的朋友！
而我知道你知道我知道你的表情说明
有些事正在撕裂你的心

告诉我，妈妈
告诉我，妈妈
告诉我，妈妈，发生了什么？
这回你是怎么啦？

喔，这编辑，我们实在是读不懂
但他彩绘的雪橇，其实是一张床
是啊，我看见你在窗台上
但是我说不清你离那个边儿有多远
而不管怎么说，你只是想要人跳和喊
你要干那种事是为什么？
因为我知道你知道我知道你知道
有些事正在撕裂你的心

---

[1] 于密林（in the woods），日美联合出品的黑泽明电影《罗生门》，其英文名即 *In the Woods*。
[2] 意语版译注认为该句无意义。

Ah, tell me, momma

Tell me, momma

Tell me, momma, what is it?

What's wrong with you this time?

啊，告诉我，妈妈
告诉我，妈妈
告诉我，妈妈，发生了什么？
这回你是怎么啦？

SHE'S YOUR LOVER NOW

The pawnbroker roared
Also, so, so did the landlord
The scene was so crazy, wasn't it?
Both were so glad
To watch me destroy what I had
Pain sure brings out the best in people, doesn't it?
Why didn't you just leave me if you didn't want to stay?
Why'd you have to treat me so bad?
Did it have to be that way?
Now you stand here expectin' me to remember somethin' you forgot to say
Yes, and you, I see you're still with her, well
That's fine 'cause she's comin' on so strange, can't you tell?
Somebody had better explain
She's got her iron chain
I'd do it, but I, I just can't remember how
You talk to her
She's your lover now

I already assumed
That we're in the felony room
But I ain't a judge, you don't have to be nice to me

她现在是你的人了

当铺老板狂笑
房东也、也、也在叫
场面太疯狂了,不是吗?
这二位如此开心
看到我毁掉了我拥有的
痛苦确实能激发出人最好的一面,不是吗?
假如你不想待了,何不干脆离开?
为何非要对我这么坏?
非得这样吗?
这会儿你站在这儿,指望我记起你忘记
　　说的事
是的,而你,我看见你仍和她在一起,呃
好吧因为她变得实在奇怪,你看不出来吗?
最好有人解释
她有她的铁索
这事儿我会做的,只是我,不记得怎么做了
你去对她说吧
她现在是你的人了

我假想过
我们是在重罪室里
但我不是法官,你没必要讨好我

But please tell that

To your friend in the cowboy hat

You know he keeps on sayin' ev'rythin' twice to me

You know I was straight with you

You know I've never tried to change you in any way

You know if you didn't want to be with me

That you could . . . didn't have to stay

Now you stand here sayin' you forgive and forget. Honey, what can I say?

Yes, you, you just sit around and ask for ashtrays, can't you reach?

I see you kiss her on the cheek ev'rytime she gives a speech

With her picture books of the pyramid

And her postcards of Billy the Kid (why must everybody bow?)

You better talk to her 'bout it

You're her lover now

Oh, ev'rybody that cares

Is goin' up the castle stairs

But I'm not up in your castle, honey

It's true, I just can't recall

San Francisco at all

I can't even remember El Paso, uh, honey

You never had to be faithful

但请你把情况

告诉你戴牛仔帽的朋友

你知道他什么事都要对我说两遍

你知道我对你很坦率

你知道我从没想过要改变你

你知道假如你不想和我在一块儿

你就可以……没必要待这儿

现在你站这儿说你已原谅并已忘记。亲爱的,我能
　　说什么?

是的,你,你,只是坐那儿要烟灰缸,
　　你够不着吗?

我见你亲她的脸,每次当她大谈起

她的金字塔画册

还有她的比利小子[1]明信片(凭什么每个人都得鞠躬?)

你最好跟她谈谈这些

你现在是她的人了

哦,在乎这事的每一位

都将爬上城堡的楼梯

但是我不在你的城堡里,亲爱的

的的确确,旧金山我完全

想不起来了

我甚至也不记得埃尔帕索,嗯,亲爱的

你用不着非得忠诚

---

[1] 比利小子,美国西部著名枪手。

I didn't want you to grieve

Oh, why was it so hard for you

If you didn't want to be with me, just to leave?

Now you stand here while your finger's goin' up my sleeve

An' you, just what do you do anyway? Ain't there nothin' you can say?

She'll be standin' on the bar soon

With a fish head an' a harpoon

An' a fake beard plastered on her brow

You'd better do somethin' quick

She's your lover now

我不想让你心痛
啊,为什么对你来说这么难
如果你不想和我待了,那就离开啊?
这会儿你站在这儿,手指伸进我的袖子
那么你,究竟要做什么?难道你不能
　　说点儿什么?
过不了一会儿她就要站在吧台上了
手里拿着鱼头和鱼叉
眉毛上粘着假胡子
你最好赶紧去做点儿什么吧
她现在是你的人了